Stories for a teen's Heart

book 2

Books in the Stories for the Heart Collection

Stories for a Teen's Heart, Book 1

Stories for a Teen's Heart, Book 2

Stories for the Extreme Teen's Heart

Journal for a Teen's Heart

Stories for the Heart, The Second Collection
(PREVIOUSLY PUBLISHED AS MORE STORIES FOR THE HEART)

Stories for the Family's Heart

Stories for a Woman's Heart

Stories for a Man's Heart

Stories for a Faithful Heart

Stories for a Mom's Heart

Stories for a Dad's Heart

Stories for a Kindred Heart

Stories for a Cheerful Heart

Christmas Stories for the Heart

Stories for a Grad's Heart

Books by Alice Gray in the Multnomah Gift Line

The Fragrance of Friendship

A Pleasant Place

Morning Coffee and Time Alone

Quiet Moments and a Cup of Tea

Gentle Is a Grandmother's Love

Once Upon a Christmas

What teens are saying about this book

These stories are a great way to cheer you up, make you laugh, make you cry, and realize that life is very precious! You'll find that you can relate to these stories too. I really enjoyed reading this book. It's great inspiration!

HEATHER SCHWARZBURG, AGE 16

Some of these stories are for a rainy day, others for when the sun comes out, and some for times when you're all alone. But most of all they're heartwarming and tear forming. Here's another book to touch your heart.

NATHAN C. NEET, AGE 17

This book is inspirational, and it shows the power of faith and love.

ERIC SCHWICKERATH, AGE 16

The stories in this book confront the daily problems that teenagers have. Every story will make you want to read the book over and over. "Awesome" sums it all up.

CHRISTINA GENG, AGE 14

These stories really show me how I can trust God more. They also help me with problems I'm going through right now.

WIL HANSEN, AGE 16

All of these stories were inspirational, uplifting, and very encouraging. I enjoyed reading each, and I know any young adult will enjoy them just like I did. I liked how the love of Christ was shown by the stories in this book!

FABIAN CLARK, AGE 18

Amusing and adventure-filled, these stories are also deep and inspirational at the same time. I especially enjoyed the stories that were written by teens.

DANIELLE STRANNIGAN, AGE 17

Don't miss out on the great stories in
Stories for a Teen's Heart, Book 1

Forget about all the bad news and get a dose of sunshine on a cloudy day. This is a teen's treasure of stories about best friends, loving families, kind-hearted strangers, and everyday heroes. Stories that will encourage you, make you laugh, look deep inside yourself, and leave you feeling good. Teens, this touch-your-heart book is definitely for us!

SHANNA STROEBEL, AGE 15

I think this book will speak well to teens' hearts. It covers all aspects of life in an encouraging way. From friends to truth, from love to hard times, it relates various lessons through stories in a user-friendly format.

SARAH MCGHEHEY, AGE 17

The stories opened me to the realization that God's miracles aren't always huge; there are many small miracles that go unnoticed by people, yet they are the great ones.

JOHN ROBERTS, AGE 17

This book, just like the other books in the Stories for the Heart collection, will have a history of changing people's lives. Just reading these stories has changed the way I look at things. It has made me think about my actions, and it has brought back many memories. I hope that it touches other people's hearts as it has mine. These stories aren't just stories; they are real life.

SHEENA LYNNELLE SHUCK, AGE 14

This is an incredible compilation of excellent stories—stories that make you want to keep reading. Some of the stories are straight from the pen of people who were recently in the news, and these people became more real. This was a highlight for me.

JEREMY MORRIS, AGE 14

Stories for a teen's Heart

book 2

Compiled by
Alice Gray

Multnomah® Publishers *Sisters, Oregon*

STORIES FOR A TEEN'S HEART, BOOK 2
published by Multnomah Publishers, Inc.

©2001 by Multnomah Publishers, Inc.
International Standard Book Number: 1-57673-797-7

Cover photos by Multnomah Publishers, Inc.
Interior illustrations by Chaz Chapman
Interior icons by Elizabeth Haidle
Interior photos by Corbis, Digital Vision,
PhotoDisc, and Multnomah Publishers, Inc.

Unless otherwise indicated, Scripture quotations are taken from:
The Holy Bible, New International Version
©1973, 1984 by International Bible Society,
used by permission of Zondervan Publishing House

Also quoted: *The Living Bible* (TLB)
©1971. Used by permission of Tyndale House Publishers, Inc.
All rights reserved.
New American Standard Bible (NASB) ©1960, 1977 by
the Lockman Foundation

Multnomah is a trademark of Multnomah Publishers, Inc.,
and is registered in the U.S. Patent and Trademark Office.

The colophon is a trademark of Multnomah Publishers, Inc.

Stories for the Heart is a trademark of Multnomah Publishers, Inc.,
and is registered in the U.S. Patent and Trademark Office.

Printed in the United States of America

For information:
MULTNOMAH PUBLISHERS, INC. • POST OFFICE BOX 1720 • SISTERS, OREGON 97759

Library of Congress Cataloging-in-Publication Data:
Stories for a teen's heart: over 100 stories to encourage a teen's
soul / compiled by Alice Gray.
        p.   cm.
    ISBN 1-57673-646-6 (alk. paper)
    1. Teenagers—Religious life Anecdotes 2. Teenagers—Conduct of
life Anecdotes.   I. Gray, Alice, 1939–
BV4531.2.S83   1999
242'.63—dc21   99-40435
                                                            CIP

01 02 03 04 05 06 07—10 9 8 7 6 5 4 3 2 1 0

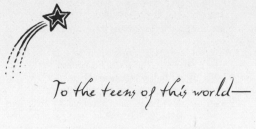

To the teens of this world—

You have been created for such a time as this.
So...
fly to the moon
shoot for the stars
rise with the morning sun
ripping apart the dark
awaking the dreams inside your heart.

KIMBER ANNIE ENGSTROM

A special thank you to...

THE AUTHORS
for writing stories that touch the hearts of teens.

CHAZ CHAPMAN
for sharing your gift of cartoon art.

STEVE GARDNER
for extraordinary cover and interior design.

JENNIFER GATES, JUDY GORDON MORROW, *and* NANCY JO SULLIVAN
for your enthusiastic support as we worked together.
You are an extraordinary team!
This labor of love isn't mine…it's ours.
It's time to celebrate with tea and chocolate!

SHELLEY MCLENDON, ERIKA POSTON, *and* LENETTE STROEBEL
for countless hours of research in libraries, bookstores, and on the Internet.
You found the best of the best!

KEVIN MARKS *and* JULEE SCHWARZBURG
for your management perspective and encouragement.

DOREEN BUTTON *and* CASANDRA LINDELL
for helping with the final selection of stories and giving us your valuable comments.

MONICA BETHEL, FABIAN CLARK, WIL HANSEN, DANAE JACOBSON,
SARAH MCGHEHEY, NATHAN NEET, RACHEL NEET, HEATHER SCHWARZBURG,
ERIC SCHWICKERATH, DANIELLE STRANNIGAN, *and* SHANNA STROEBEL
for sharing your teen perspective.
Your enthusiasm and support cheered us on.

AL GRAY
for always believing in me.

Contents

Reach for the Stars

With You All the Way

Forever Friends

Love's All in the Family

Keep Looking Up

Yeah, You Make a Difference

Attitude Check

You Know What's Right

Hang in There

It's a God Thing

Reach for the Stars

When you have tomorrow in your heart
you never run out of dreaming room.
And dreaming is the stuff of hope.

JEAN PIERRE GODET

I'm Still Here

MARY HOLLINGSWORTH
FROM *HUGS FOR WOMEN*

The day before registration at college, Janice—a pretty red-haired freshman—arrived in town by bus. Carrying her single worn suitcase, held closed with an old belt because the clasps had broken, she walked the four miles from the Greyhound station to the campus on the east side of town. Janice wandered around campus for a few minutes, just looking at the buildings with amazement. She couldn't believe she was really there. In spite of all the struggles in her life, she had finally made it.

Smiling to herself, Janice went to the administration building and climbed the giant staircase to the front doors. She pulled the huge oak door open and slowly walked down the hall, taking in the sights and smells. Finally finding the right door, she straightened her skirt, brushed back her hair, and walked into the office. Pearl, longtime administrative aide to the president of the college, looked up and smiled.

"I'd like to see the president, please," said Janice with confidence.

"Won't you have a seat?" asked Pearl. "I'll just see if he's off the phone."

Soon Janice was shown into the president's office. Nervous but determined, she set her suitcase down and blurted out, "Sir, I'm here to go to school. I have my clothes and eighteen dollars. That's all. I can't go back home because I don't have enough money to get there. But I can work; I can work hard. And I'm capable of learning anything I need to learn. I want to go to school here more than anything else in the world. Can you help me?"

The president smiled. He was a warm-hearted, robust man who loved college kids…especially determined ones. "Yes, I think I can," he grinned. And help her he did, by arranging financial aid, on-campus jobs, and scholarships.

That night, Janice called her mother. "Mama, I'm here. And I get to stay! I'm going to school!"

Then for four hard years, Janice cleaned food trays in the cafeteria, mopped floors in the student center, carried huge stacks of books to be refiled in the library, hauled trash out of the administration building, and did numerous other less-than-glamorous jobs. When Janice wasn't working, she was in class or studying.

Unlike most of us on campus, Janice didn't get to join in most of the social activities on campus. She had no free time. She didn't go to parties; she didn't date; she didn't join a social club; she didn't go to the movies on Friday nights. She just worked and studied, studied and worked. And she smiled a lot.

"Hey, Janice, how's it going?" we'd ask.

"Great! With God's help, I'm still here!" she'd say and laugh as she scraped the food off yet another cafeteria tray.

During our senior year, the Hong Kong flu descended on campus with a vengeance. At one point, more than half the four thousand kids in school had the flu. Between her regular jobs, Janice went from room to room in her dorm, helping the nurse take care of the sick girls, cleaning up after them, bringing them medicine and liquids. For two solid weeks she hardly slept.

Then, just as almost everyone was getting well, the flu hit Janice hard. In spite of Janice's protests that she had to go to work, the nurse put her to bed. "But I can't afford to miss work," she moaned. "I need every dollar I earn to stay in school."

When the girls in Janice's dorm heard she was sick, they quickly went into action to repay her kindness. One friend reported to the cafeteria to scrape trays; one went to the administration building and hauled out the trash; another mopped the floors in the student center; and still another pulled her shift refiling books in the library. And they took turns doing it every day while Janice got well. When Janice returned to work, her time cards showed that she had worked four hours overtime during the week she was sick!

Janice and I graduated the same day. When I walked across the stage, I quietly received my diploma. When Janice walked onto the stage a few minutes later, the entire student body rose to its feet and cheered (something that just wasn't done at solemn graduation ceremonies in those days). She had earned our great respect and admiration.

Amazed at the uncharacteristic cheering, the president stopped the formal procession and invited Janice to respond to her classmates. Surprised, but happy, Janice walked to the podium, held up her diploma, and said six words: "With God's help, I'm still here!"

The Letter

SARAH ROSE

I knew what I was looking for. Boosting myself up on a step stool, I stretched high to explore the plastic boxes stacked on my closet shelf.

It was my twenty-third birthday. My shelves were cluttered with college textbooks, scrapbooks, and countless boxes filled with cherished photos of friends.

I reached for a locked metal strongbox. Next to the small chest was a tiny canister that contained a key to the box.

As I sat down on my bed, the box in my hands, I felt my heart pound with anticipation.

A decade earlier, when I was thirteen, I had written a letter to myself. In the letter, I had included thoughts about myself and my life at that time. I had vowed not to open it until ten years had passed.

I took a deep breath and slowed my pounding heart.

As I unlocked the box, I found the journal pages I had written so many years earlier.

"To my dear sweet self," the letter said.

"Please do not open until you are twenty-three years old...This letter comes to you from the past...Happy memories," it read.

I smiled. I hardly remembered the words I had scribbled on the paper. I couldn't wait to read on:

"Right now I'm not very popular. Every day I spend my lunch hour at school sulking in the girls' locker room. I think I'm waiting for someone to come and spend time with me. I'd settle for one friend. The popular kids don't like me. Sometimes they make me cry. They think I'm ugly. I think I'm ugly, too. Are you pretty? Do you have a boyfriend? I wish I did.

"I have dreams for the future. Right now I hope to be an English teacher or a poet or maybe someone who helps others.

"I believe in God. Even in the rough times, I know that He's always with me. When you get this letter, please write back. Who did you grow up to be?

"Sincerely yours,

"Your Dear Sweet Self."

For a moment, I sat in silence, keenly aware that the thirteen-year-old girl was still a part of me. I wanted to share so much with her.

I took a tablet and a pen from a bedside table and began to answer her letter.

"To my Dear Sweet Self," I began.

"This letter comes to you from your future. Today I'm celebrating twenty-three years of life. Though the last ten years have not always been easy, I am happy to report that I have learned a great deal. Let me summarize my experiences.

"In high school, I struggled with liking myself. I worked hard at fitting in with the popular group, but I never managed to become 'cool.' Nonetheless, I had the great fortune of finding one true friend. Despite my insecurities and lack of self-esteem, my friend stood by me. She always told me that beauty comes from within. She was right. After high school, I went on to college and learned how to teach handicapped children. I graduated with honors. In just one month I will begin my first teaching assignment. I'm looking forward to being a friend to the unpopular of the world,—the blind, the deaf, the mentally challenged. I can't wait to affirm their inner beauty. I want to remind my students that they are created in God's image and likeness.

"You mentioned in your letter that you wanted me to tell you who I grew up to be. Well, I grew up to be a very wise woman. I now know that life holds many struggles, but that God brings good out of every hardship.

"I know that friendship can never be dependent on appearance but on love freely shared. And I know that true beauty resides in the human heart, and that I was and always will be extremely beautiful.

"As I close this letter, I will also close my eyes. I want to imagine myself giving you a big hug.

"I'm proud of you, Sarah.

"Sincerely,

Your Dear Sweet Self."

Dreams are reached by facing obstacles and climbing hills.

SARAH MCGHEHEY

The Mark of a Champion

MARILYN K. MCAULEY

John, a gymnastic specialist on still rings, was waiting to execute his routine at the districtwide meet. It was his first year to have a chance at going to state. To do this, he had to place in one of the top six scores. The pressure was on to score well for both his team and himself.

John rubbed the chalk dust into his hands in preparation for mounting the rings. Once on the mat, he respectfully acknowledged the judges and offered up a prayer. He had done his part in learning and perfecting the moves, now he trusted the Lord to enable him to do his best. Strong and muscular, he took to still rings like a monkey to a limb. It was his sport.

Two years earlier, John had dropped into the gymnastics gym to watch as the fellows practiced their moves. One of the gymnasts completed a back-up rise and upon dismounting, John asked, "Can I try to do that?"

"Sure."

John dusted his hands with chalk and walked over to the rings. With an assist, he was up and executing the move he had just observed.

"Man! You ever done that before?" the gymnast asked, incredulous over the ease with which John did the move.

John assured him he hadn't.

"You're a natural. You gotta get on the team!"

As a junior a year later at the district meet, John was a real asset to his team but he never felt overconfident. This was an important moment. He didn't want to blow it.

Coach gave him the assist to mount the rings and then stood by to spot for him. John's muscles rippled as he hoisted himself into position. From his first move through his bailout, he executed each move to the best of his ability. Landing with a solid dismount he felt he had a chance at going to state. He acknowledged the judges again and left the mat.

They waited for the judges to score. Silence. A long silence, Finally, the gymnasts and their scores flashed on, revealing that John had taken sixth place. *Yes!* He was going to state. However, when all of the scores for the still ring event were posted, John discovered that his score had been exchanged with the seventh place gymnast, a fellow teammate, now placing John in seventh position.

Coach hurried over to talk with the judges, then he talked to John. "Some technical glitch has put you in seventh place. The judges think they're right, but I believe they made an error. I protested but want you to have a part in the outcome. Do you want me to protest again for sixth place? Remember, it means not going to state if you accept seventh place."

John knew Coach would do anything he could for him. He was that way with his gymnasts. He thought a moment. *I know winning isn't everything. My teammate is a senior—it's his last chance to go to state.* Finally he said, "Leave it alone, Coach. He's a senior. I have another year."

John never regretted his decision.

Through his senior year, he worked hard. He was chosen captain of the varsity and won one competition after another. He qualified for All American throughout the year, which means a score of 8.8 or 9 for a minimum of four meets. John qualified in every meet that year. When district meets came up again that next spring, John took first and finally got to go on to state.

His nerves were taut as he entered the college gymnasium that day. All the competing teams from around the state were there. He wondered where he stood with those he had never seen perform.

His final performance was next to last and pitted him against a fellow from another school in his city. Having competed against him a number of times over the three years, he knew what he was up against. This kid was good!

John's turn was up. Hands dusted with chalk, he stood near the rings and acknowledged the judges, then positioned himself for the assist from Coach.

Strength and concentration showed as he hoisted himself into a front pull-up followed by a routine of the most difficult moves and ending with a pike bailout. His dismount was a solid plant of his feet on the mat. He did it! He acknowledged the judges again and left the mat to the cheers of his family and friends in the grandstand. John knew he had accomplished his best performance ever, but would it be the winning performance?

His stiffest competitor mounted the rings. John watched his every move. It seemed flawless and John began to wonder. Suddenly, he bungled a move. At that moment one of the coaches standing next to John said, "Congratulations, champ!" When the gymnast hopped on his dismount, John knew he really was the new Oregon State Still Rings Champion.

A year before he had shown the heart of a champion. A year later, he had the medal to prove it.

I Am Loni

CYNTHIA HAMOND

Why do I even try? If there's one thing I should have learned, it's try or not, I'll probably screw up. Mom says, "Loni, a lady shouldn't say things like 'screwed up.'" That just proves my point. I even screw up how to tell you that I screwed up.

I know, I have so much going for me. Don't even go there. Dad brags about my grades and Mom's proud of the person I am and all my church activities. Grandma goes on and on about my pretty face. *Yeah, too bad about the rest of me,* I think to myself.

I'm not like big enough to be featured as The Amazing Amazon Teen in *The Guinness Book of World Records,* but I am big enough not to like shopping with my friends. "How cu-u-u-u-ute!" They squeal over every rack of clothes. They know they'll fit into anything. I can't commit until I scan the plastic circle dividers to see how high the sizes go.

I pretend that clothes don't matter to me. That explains my semi-grunge look everyone takes for my chosen style. No outfit is complete without a sweater, flannel, or sweatshirt tied around my waist to cover up...oh...everything.

So, when we go to the mall, I'm the designated shopper. You know, like the designated driver, they go to a party but don't partake. I stand outside the changing rooms to ooh and aah when they emerge for the three-way mirror check. Only after a careful inspection or it would be taken as insincere, I reassure them that their thighs, legs, waist, or bottom do not look too big in that outfit.

It takes all I have not to roll my eyes when they hand me a piece of clothing and plead, "Can you see if this comes a size smaller?" Give me a break. Where should I look? The children's department?

I really did screw up, though. Being a self-appointed good sport, I tried out for the volleyball team with my friends. Here's the bad part: I made it.

It seems I have a killer serve. I use it for self-defense. The harder I ram the ball, the less likely it will be returned and force me to clod around the court keeping it in play.

To make matters worse, we kept winning. This was the first winning season of any girls' sport in our school's history. Volleyball fever took over and attendance soared. Just my luck. The more the merrier, I never say. And those pep rallies. There's a thrill. Jumping around high-fiving while my name echoes over the PA system.

In our small town, making it to state finals is newsworthy. Our team was pictured sitting in the bleachers in a V for victory formation. I was the connecting bottom of the V—front and center in all my glory.

No, this isn't the golden moment when seeing myself in the paper, I realize I had miraculously become a lovely swan. Believe me, if I'd been transformed, I would have noticed.

Truthfully, I didn't think the picture was all that bad. I studied the smiles of the girls sitting behind me. It wasn't them and, oh yeah, that Loni too. We were friends, we were a team, and I was an important part of it. I liked that. I was just fine, being who I was, doing what I was doing.

"Loni Leads the Charge to State!" read the headline. Not bad. I didn't even pretend to protest when Mom bought copies for the relatives. I was pleased when the team framed the picture and hung it in the tunnel between our locker room and the arena. It soon became our team gesture to blow kisses at our picture every time we passed it.

The night of the final game came and we had home court advantage. The series was tied two games to two. I led the team's run for our triumphant entrance. Cheers stormed down the tunnel to meet us. We glanced at the banners posted along the walls taking energy from the words.

YOU GO, GIRLS!

YES, YOU CAN!

WE'RE #1!

We were ready to blow kisses at our picture when shock froze me. Two words were written in red on the glass. Two words that totally changed the headline.

"Loni THE BULL Leads the Charge to State!"

The horns drawn on my head completed the insult.

I felt myself emptying until I wasn't me anymore. I was nobody. The team bunched behind me.

"Who did this?"

"Who would be so mean?"

Their questions had no answers. They thought they were as upset as I was, but they were wrong. I wasn't upset at all. I was flat.

So this is the truth, I thought. *This is who I am.*

And all the words around me didn't heal the hurt because nobody said the three words I most needed to hear: "That's not true."

The team moved me down the tunnel. There was no time to sort myself. What was real seemed like a dream and I couldn't shake myself awake. The chants of "Loni! Loni!" sounded hollow. I let the cheers of the many be muted by the jeers of the few.

We won the coin toss and took to the court for my first serve. Around me the team was pumped and ready to go. I rolled the volleyball in my palms to get its feel and mechanically went into my serving stance. All I could see were the words...THE BULL...THE BULL...THE BULL.

I tossed the ball up, but before my fist made contact the shout "Olé!" hit me. I stutter stepped and missed the ball. I told myself not to look but my eyes were drawn anyway. I couldn't pick out who it was. The team tried to buck me up with the back slaps and that's okays. It didn't help.

I went through the rotations until I was at the net. My concentration scurried between the game and the bleachers. When the ball skimmed the air above my head, a loud snorting sound came from the front row.

"That's taking the bull by the horns!" someone yelled. The player behind me made the save and set up the ball for me to spike. But I wasn't looking at the ball. I was staring into the faces of the five high school boys who were mocking me. My humiliation only fueled their taunts.

"Give me a B, give me a U, give me a double L too. What's that smell? LONI! LONI! LONI!"

Why didn't someone shut them up?

The coach called a time-out. "Loni, can you get your head in the game?"

I shrugged.

"Why are you letting a few people who don't even know you decide for you who you are?"

I shrugged again.

"Loni, you're valuable as a person and to your team. Unkind words don't change who you are unless you decide they change you."

Sounds good in theory, I thought, *but this is the real world.*

"I'm keeping you in but if you can't work this through, I'll pull you."

I nodded.

I walked past the boys to take my place in the game. With each step I took, they stomped their feet to shake the floor. I got the point. Very funny.

I also had to walk past my teammates, and in spite of my weak showing they were still rooting for me.

"You can do it."

"You're the best."

Something in me gave way. The quote on a magnet on my Grandma's refrigerator popped into my thoughts. "God don't make no junk."

I knew what I knew, and I knew myself and I wasn't junk. I felt my value to the very depths of me and that value came from God. I was created in His image, after all.

Whose image of me was I? Some immature boys who only knew me from the outside? Or those who cared about me, the God who created me, and the person I knew I was?

And just like that I was free of them. Oh, they continued to stomp their feet with each of my steps. I didn't like it but it didn't matter. They were powerless in my life.

The game was close and we played hard. The winning serve fell to me. It was my moment and the real me took it. The ball went up, my fist came forward and hit right on. It was a perfect power serve unreturnable by the other team. And as the saying goes, the crowd went wild. The pep band started beating out our school song. The team huddled around me. They didn't lift me on their shoulders for the victory lap but...I'll leave that alone.

Shouts of "Loni, Loni" vibrated the arena. The funny thing is the cheers didn't feed me like they used to. They were great, but the joy I felt, the freedom I felt, the sense of myself I had come to, filled me more than any cheers.

So, we find ourselves back to my first question. Why do I even try?

Because I know I am from God. I am wonderfully made. I am Loni.

Go confidently in the direction of your dreams.

HENRY DAVID THOREAU

Risking Much

To laugh is to risk appearing the fool.
To weep is to risk appearing sentimental.
To reach out for another is to risk involvement.
To expose feelings is to risk exposing our true self.
To place your ideas, your dreams, before the crowd is to risk loss.
To love is to risk not being loved in return.
To live is to risk dying.
To hope is to risk despair.
To try at all is to risk failure.
But risk we must, because the greatest hazard in life is to risk nothing. The man, the woman, who risks nothing does nothing, has nothing, is nothing.

JAMES S. HEWETT
FROM *ILLUSTRATIONS UNLIMITED*

If the Dream Is Big Enough, the Facts Don't Count

CYNTHIA STEWART-COPIER

used to watch her from my kitchen window and laugh. She seemed so small as she muscled her way through the crowd of boys on the playground. The school was across the street from our home, and I often stood at my window, hands buried in dishwater or cookie dough, watching the kids as they played during recess. A sea of children, and yet to me, she stood out from them all.

I remember the first day I saw her playing basketball. I watched in wonder as she ran circles around the other kids. She managed to shoot jump shots just over their heads and into the net. The boys always tried to stop her, but no one could.

I began to notice her at other times, on that same blacktop, basketball in hand, playing alone. She practiced dribbling and shooting over and over again, sometimes until dark. One day I asked her why she practiced so much. As she turned her head, her dark ponytail whipped quickly around, and she looked directly into my eyes. Without hesitating, she said, "I want to go to college. My dad wasn't able to go to college, and he has talked to me about going for as long as I can remember. The only way I can go is if I get a scholarship. I like basketball. I decided that if I were good enough, I would get a scholarship. I am going to play college basketball. I want to be the best. My daddy told me if the dream is big enough, the facts don't count." Then she smiled and ran toward the court to recap the routine I had seen over and over again.

Well, I had to give it to her—she was determined. I watched her through those junior high years and into high school. Every week, she led her varsity team to victory. It was always a thrill to watch her play.

One day in her senior year, I saw her sitting in the grass, head cradled in her arms. I walked across the street and sat down beside her. Quietly I asked what was wrong.

"Oh, nothing," came a soft reply. "I am just too short." The coach had told her that at five feet, five inches tall, she would probably never get to play for a top-ranked team—much less be offered a scholarship—so she should stop dreaming about college.

She was heartbroken, and I felt my own throat tighten as I sensed her disappointment. I asked her if she had talked to her dad about it yet.

She lifted her head from her hands and told me that her father said those coaches were wrong. They just did not understand the power of a dream. He told her that if she really wanted to play for a good college, if she truly wanted a scholarship, that nothing could stop her except one thing—her own attitude. He told her again, "If the dream is big enough, the facts don't count."

The next year, as she and her team went to the Northern California championship game, she was seen by a college recruiter who was there to watch the opposing team. She was indeed offered a scholarship, a full ride, to an NCAA Division I women's basketball team. She accepted. She was going to get the college education that she had dreamed of and worked toward for all those years. And that little girl had more playing time as a freshman and sophomore than any other woman in the history of that university.

Late one night during her junior year of college, her father called her. "I'm sick, honey. I have cancer. No, don't quit school and come home. Everything will be okay. I love you."

He died six weeks later—her hero, her dad. She did leave school those last few days to support her mother and care for her father. Late one night during the final hours before his death, he called for her in the darkness.

As she came to his side, he reached for her hand and struggled to speak. "Rachel, keep dreaming. Don't let your dream die with me. Promise me," he pleaded. "Promise me."

In those last few precious moments together, she replied, "I promise, Daddy."

Those years to follow were hard on her. She was torn between school and her family, knowing her mother was left alone with a new baby and three other children to raise. The grief she felt over the loss of her father was always there, hidden in that place she kept inside, waiting to raise its head at some unsuspecting moment and drop her again to her knees.

Everything seemed harder. She struggled daily with fear, doubt, and frustration. A severe learning disability had forced her to go to school year-round for three years just to keep up with requirements. The testing facility on campus couldn't believe she had made it through even one semester. Every time she wanted to quit she remembered her father's words: "Rachel, keep dreaming. Don't let your dream die. If the dream is big enough, you can do anything! I believe in you." And, of course, she remembered the promise she made to him.

My daughter kept her promise and completed her degree. It took her six years, but she did not give up. She can still be found sometimes as the sun sets, bouncing a basketball. And often I hear her tell others, "If the dream is big enough, the facts don't count."

The Impossible Dream

SANDY AUSTIN

What? Do you think I'm a failure, too? Of course I want to graduate with my class!" A tear rolled down Brandi's cheek. "Everyone's always getting on my case, but no one knows what it's like to live in my skin!" Tears flooded her eyes, and her steely presence melted into the chair.

"Brandi, what do you want—not what does your mom or dad want for you, but what do you want?"

Brandi replied hopelessly, "I want to graduate with the class of 2000!"

Four F's out of six classes—Brandi's report card screamed "failure." As a school counselor, I had heard it over and over again by kids failing most of their classes. Once more I wanted to believe this student could make it. Brandi should be an eleventh grader, but her credits said she was almost a year behind because of all the classes she failed. Her graduating class would be the class of 2000—the first one of the new millennium. She wanted to make history with them.

Looking back, Brandi had a great ninth grade year—passing all her classes and fitting in with the cool crowd at school. Then her parents divorced, and Brandi was shipped to live with her dad out of town. In turmoil, Brandi couldn't fit in at the new school. Deadening loneliness drove her to hang out with the wrong crowd. Ditching school, driving fast cars, and experimenting with drugs and alcohol became a part of Brandi's life. After failing all her classes, she was sent to live in our area with her mom.

Flashing an attitude, Brandi enrolled at our school in the fall of her junior year. Fear seeped through her iron-clad demeanor, and I could tell she was scared about starting a new school again. We discussed the clubs and activities at school that could help her feel connected, but I knew she lacked confidence.

Nine weeks later she was in my office again with four F's on her report card. "Why are you ditching those classes?" I asked her. I could see that fear was creeping in again.

We talked and she came up with a plan to pass three of those classes. Her confidence was building, and it skyrocketed later when she passed. "Miss Austin, I did it!" she screeched as she threw me a high five. She began to believe in herself.

I encouraged her to become a student assistant in the counseling office so I could see her daily. She needed to know someone believed in her. I saw a lot of potential in her, and I wanted to help her see that too. "Hey, Miss Austin, what's up?" was her greeting each time we could sit and talk. She became our best student assistant, and her attendance in other classes was almost perfect.

Brandi had a longing to be in sports, but her home situation always prevented it. I encouraged her to go out for the volleyball team, but she knew it would almost be impossible to make the team as a senior. She started working out.

That spring semester Brandi passed all her classes and was now a little more than a semester behind on credits the summer before her senior year. She knew she had to go to summer school—but eight classes! That meant she would have to be in school every day of the summer and not have a summer break.

During this time I was offered a job at another school for the next year. I was concerned that Brandi would give up, since I was her support and encouragement at the school. We had long talks about it that spring. I told her I would be praying for her every day during the summer.

When the new school year started, I still hadn't heard from Brandi. I wondered if she made it through summer school. Then one day I got her letter. I ripped it open:

Miss Austin,

I'm sorry it has taken me so long to write, but I just wanted to wait so I could tell you that I made varsity in volleyball and that I did make it through summer school. I have proved to myself and everyone else that I am able to take on the responsibility of my own actions. You will be happy to know that I didn't skip one day of summer school. I was there every single day. It was hard, but I hung in there and got through it all.

I just want to thank you for being there for me and for believing in me. You have made a big difference in my life, because you are someone that really cares. Thank you so much. Well, I hope everything goes good for you at your new school and I hope they treat you good. The kids will really look up to you like I do. Maybe you can help someone there like you have helped me. Thank you so much for everything; you mean a lot to me, really.

Always,

Brandi

Class of 2000

Months later Brandi strode across the stage and, thrusting her fists into the air, she yelled, "I did it!" as she received her diploma with the class of 2000. A tear rolled down my cheek.

More Than a Picasso

STEPHANIE SPARKMAN

iwas eighteen years old, and I was determined it was time to spread my wings, to set out on my own, to get my own place.

So, this particular art show was more fun than most. I looked around with my most critical eye for just the right piece to put in the new apartment I was going to rent.

Many of the pieces I saw were beautiful, but far too expensive for someone with more dreams than money. However, one picture caught my eye. It was a bright yellow sun in a faded red frame—fairly abstract, more cartoon than art. A face was painted on the sun...blue eyes, big red mouth, turned upward in a smile. It was happy, and looking at it made me happy.

A name was scrawled in the bottom left corner: Billy Williams.

Stepping back a little to study it further, I told myself I'd never spend money on a painting like that, because, after all, I could paint one just like it if I really wanted one. There didn't seem to be a lot of artistic talent, and, in fact, it looked like a child had done it. If a child could do something that caught my attention, I could do the same thing, only better!

Yeah. That's what I'd do. I'd paint my own sun picture!

As I began to move away from the booth, something caught my ear. Was someone talking to me? I didn't see anyone.

I stopped and looked at the picture again. This time, I saw a fellow in a wheelchair trying to get my attention.

"Like it?" I thought I heard him ask.

It was hard for me to hear him. The tent was crowded and very loud. I moved closer to him.

"Do I like it? Yes, I really do, but…"

He started talking again, but it was hard for me to understand him. He talked very softly and slowly, drawing his words out to the point where my mind had a hard time following them.

"I liiiiike to paaaaaint," he said.

"Really?" I asked, noticing for the first time that there were many other paintings in his booth.

"I like your paintings very much." I continued. "How do you come up with so many things to paint?"

"It's eeeeasy," he replied. "Aaaanyone can dooooo it. All youuuu have to dooooo is get an ideeeeea in your heeeead, deciiiiide what you waaant to do, and dooooo it."

He then shared with me how he had painted the sun picture. The entire conversation took about fifteen minutes. Fifteen painful minutes. As he struggled to get the words out and I struggled to understand them, I learned a lesson I have never forgotten.

"How much for this painting?" I asked.

"Fiiiiive dollaaaaars," was the reply.

I gave him the five dollars, put my prize under my arm, and left.

It had taken Billy Williams fifteen painful minutes to teach me a lesson I've kept close to my heart for the following twenty-eight years. This awkward-looking young man, hands gnarled, legs twisted, tongue thick, had broken the code on a part of life I hadn't even known existed.

The man who made one of the greatest impacts on my life is someone who will never know it. I've never seen him again.

He would never be able to overcome his physical challenges, but he had learned to deal with them. He had learned that doing what he wanted to do was simply a matter of getting an idea, deciding what he wanted the outcome to look like, and making it happen.

He said anyone could do it. He was right.

The Shoestring

BOB WELCH

FROM *STORIES FROM THE GAME OF LIFE*

He was a no-name kid lost amid big-name athletes, a twenty-two-year-old runner from Atlanta named Tim Willis who was competing far from home. He was an 800-meter guy. And he was in Eugene, Oregon, on this mild June evening in 1993 to run in the USA/Mobil Track and Field Championships at the University of Oregon's Hayward Field.

Reporter's notebook in hand, I stood at trackside. Willis's race began. As the runners in the two-lap event spaced themselves out, Willis quickly fell to the back of the pack. After half a lap he was about five yards behind the leaders. After a full lap, about ten.

Had this been Hollywood, Willis would have run the bell lap like an inspired sprinter, lunged at the finish line to win, and later found himself surrounded by reporters and autograph seekers. He would have been the hero of the day. And when he awoke the next morning at the Hilton, the newspaper left in front of his room would have been emblazoned with his photo.

Instead, Tim Willis finished dead last. His time, two minutes and ten seconds, wouldn't have won most high school meets. I watched as he sat in the infield, putting on his sweats. Not far away, reporters and autograph seekers crowded around pentathlete Jackie Joyner-Kersee.

Sometimes, courage lives in the shadows. On this night at least, it did. On this night it lived in the heart of a young man named Tim Willis. There is nothing particularly noteworthy, you see, in running 800 meters in two minutes and ten seconds.

Unless you're blind.

He was ten when it happened: Coats' Disease, a hemorrhaging of the retina. Within three years, Tim Willis's vision was completely gone. In junior high, he started wrestling, which required running. The high school cross-country coach saw him run and invited him to come out for the team.

Why not?

Willis learned to stay on course with the help of a shoestring tether he shared with a guide, who ran beside him. The guide would say something like, "Ditch coming up. Three, two, one, ditch!" Tim averaged about one fall per race, but nothing worse than skinned knees.

By the time he was a senior in high school, Willis was scoring points as one of his high school's top five runners. But with him now making a difference in team results, the Georgia High School Association ruled him ineligible to run. Being tethered to a guide, they said, gave him an advantage that other runners didn't have. It broke the rules.

Willis was crushed. But after the story ran on the front page of the *Atlanta Constitution,* calls of support for Willis poured in from around the country. *USA Today* picked up the story. Willis was on national TV. And the athletic association overturned its ruling.

Tim Willis ran on in the darkness.

On the day before his race in Eugene, I met Tim Willis at the university dorm he was staying in across from Hayward Field. Reporters generally ask the questions, but instead Willis led off with one for me. Would I be willing to drive him to the spot where distance runner Steve Prefontaine had died?

Minutes later, we were there, on Hendricks Hill just east of the University of Oregon campus. I watched as Willis's hands felt the contours of a rocky wall along a narrow twisting lane. All was quiet, except for an occasional bird chirping and the distant whir of Interstate 5.

"MPre 5-30-75 RIP" someone had painted on the rock.

I talked of how Prefontaine had been my hero while I was a young runner. Willis talked of how even though Pre had died when Tim was four years old, the Oregon runner became his hero, too. "What I admired about him was the way he could come back," Willis said. "After finishing fourth at Munich, a lot of people might have given up. He bounced back and set his sights on '76."

What I admired about Tim Willis was that he ran at all. Watching him race the next night, I was reminded that courage isn't measured with a stopwatch, but in one's willingness to take risk. And humility to trust.

We often find ourselves alone on that starting line. Unable to see. Blind to whatever lies ahead. Destined, it might seem, to fail.

Which is where faith comes into play. Faith is more than about running in the darkness; it's about being willing to trust someone else to lead us through that darkness.

It's about dropping our pride and, in humility, admitting we can't do it on our own.

It's about tethering ourselves to the God who longs to be our guide and letting Him lead.

Faith it seems is born of courage. It has nothing to do with the eyes. And, as Tim Willis taught me that summer night, everything to do with the heart.

Welcome to Heaven

TIM SULLIVAN AS TOLD TO NANCY JO SULLIVAN
FROM *MOMENTS OF GRACE*

Back in the winter of 1969, when I was a little boy, my dad and I made an ice-skating rink in our backyard. Set against the frozen Minnesota moonlight, I held a garden hose with mittened hands, the water freezing on its way to the ground.

My dad stood by, a six-foot-four-inch giant in a puffy down jacket.

"It's like heaven out here," he said.

I looked upward, following Dad's gaze to a starlit sky. My toes were numb, curling inside my boots. My water soaked mittens were growing a thin coat of ice.

"Heaven?" I asked. I didn't know what he meant.

The winter weeks passed while Dad and I spent many nights skating together on that homemade rink. While wind chills dipped well below zero, Dad taught me how to grip a hockey stick and how to "slap shoot" a puck. Beneath a snowy firmament, Dad and I would glide around a makeshift net made of shovels and sheets, the metal blades of our skates etching curly lines on the ice.

"C'mon. Shoot it! Go for a breakaway! Don't hit the goalpost!" Dad would shout, his voice echoing against the snowbanks.

He was loud. At times he was gruff. But at the end of every evening, as we gathered up equipment, Dad would quiet himself, lifting his eyes to the sky.

I knew that Dad stored the Lord in his heart, but he seldom used words to express that faith. This nightly reflection was a prayer of sorts, a way of showing me that God was important.

One night, I got tired of waiting for him to finish up his intercessions. I was cold, and Mom had hot chocolate waiting for us in the kitchen.

"It'll feel like heaven when we get inside," I yelled, trying to pry him away from his winter worship.

Dad chuckled as he pulled off my stocking cap and started tickling me. We laughed all the way to the kitchen door.

Winter after winter, Dad was by my side, helping me to perfect the game. He taught me how to speed skate around orange construction cones, how to pass a puck, how to guard a goalpost.

By the time I made captain of our high school hockey team, Dad was content to watch me from the sides of a new arena.

At the state tournament, as I scored the winning goal, the standing room only crowd began to clap and cheer.

But I skated past the crowded bleachers, racing my way to the goalpost. There, behind a sheet of Plexiglas, Dad stood alone. I tapped the glass with my stick as Dad gave me a thumbs-up.

"Heaven!" he shouted.

As my high school years came to a close, I signed scholarship papers to attend Providence College in Rhode Island. The school was miles away from Minnesota.

It was an honor to wear the Providence uniform. I made a lot of friends and played against the best hockey teams in the country.

Every week, I'd write Dad, sending him team programs and newspaper clippings. "I'm having a great time," I would write.

But the truth was, I'd get homesick whenever I skated in unfamiliar arenas. The space behind the goalpost was always empty.

Then one Friday night in March 1985, Providence played Michigan State, a national championship game.

Before the game, as I laced up my skates, my coach told me I had a visitor waiting outside the locker room. It was my dad.

"Hey," I said, greeting him with a friendly punch in the arm.

"Not too bad a drive from Minnesota," my father quipped.

Standing in my skates, suited in shoulder pads and thick breezers, I suddenly realized I was looking down on him.

He lingered for a while, trying to put his thought into words.

"The good Lord is proud of you," he said, patting me on the back. It was seldom that I heard Dad talk like this.

"The good Lord is proud of you too," I replied.

The game began. As I skated past the cheering crowds, I searched for Dad behind the goalpost, but found him sitting with my mom in the bleachers, right behind the players' bench.

As our eyes met, he pointed to a banner posted high above the rink— it spanned the entire arena.

Intended to highlight the superior skill and strength of the opposing team, the banner read: "Welcome to Heaven."

I laughed to myself as the referee dropped the puck to begin the opening face-off.

The crowd roared. Minute by minute, Providence maintained a two-point lead with Michigan State. With five minutes left in the game, I scored a goal.

Looking up toward the bleachers where Dad was sitting, I expected to see him give me a thumbs-up. Instead, I saw the team chaplain and a doctor huddled over him. There was a look of shock on my mom's face.

As an ambulance pulled up in front of an entryway that overlooked the goalpost, my coach ushered me through the jammed crowd.

Dad died fifteen minutes after I arrived at the hospital.

When the team chaplain comforted my mom, I slipped away to a large lobby window. Still clad in my skates and uniform, I watched a snow shower blanket the city. I began to recount the last few hours.

How fitting it seemed that a "Welcome to Heaven" banner had decorated the arena where Dad had passed away.

I was certain that eternity was now his inheritance, a reward for teaching me about the love of God.

He taught me about this love, not so much in well-spoken words, but in the time he spent with me. Throughout the years, Dad had stood by my side, like an ever-present heavenly Father, teaching me how to perfect the game of life.

How to share laughter.

How to offer the gift of "presence."

How to pray without uttering a sound.

As I stood there, a passage from Matthew's gospel came to mind: "The kingdom of heaven is near" (Matthew 3:2).

I understood a little better that the love between a father and a son is a bit of heaven on earth.

With You
All the Way

We are like angels with just one wing.
We fly only by embracing each other.

AUTHOR UNKNOWN

The Paper Cup

DANA GIESE

One night I was sitting in my kitchen half-listening as my fifteen-year-old brother Tommy antagonized my twelve-year-old brother Kevin. I didn't pay attention when Kevin charged up the stairs with a hurt look on his face.

About twenty minutes later, as I was heading upstairs, I heard Kevin crying inside the bathroom. I bit my tongue to stop myself from saying, "Come on, Kev, don't be such a baby." Instead, I knocked on the door and asked, "Hey, Kev, do you wanna talk?"

No response.

I tried again, "Hey, why don't you come out of there?"

Again, no response.

So, joking around, I grabbed a stack of index cards and a pencil and wrote, "If you don't want to talk, we can write notes to each other."

An hour later I was still sitting on the floor outside the bathroom with two stacks of index cards in front of me. One was blank and one was cards from Kevin on which he had translated all his yucky feelings into words for me. By this time I didn't care about all the rings of my precious phone or my favorite show downstairs. As I read one of Kevin's notes, tears came to my eyes. It said, "Nobody in this family cares about me. I'm not the youngest, and I'm not the oldest, and I'm not talented. Tommy thinks I'm a wuss, and Dad wishes he had the other Kevin as a kid because he's better at basketball. And you're never around to notice me."

Tears came to my eyes as I read his words. It was true what he had said about me. I wrote back, "You know, Kev, I really do love you, and I'm sorry I don't always show it. I am here for you, and you are loved in this family."

There was no response for a while, but then I heard a tearing sound coming from inside the bathroom. Kevin, who had run out of index cards, wrote on a torn-up paper cup, "Thanks."

I wrote back, "For what?" It returned to me with "Loving me" written on it.

Since then, I try my best to never only half notice my family members anymore. Kevin and I have a closer relationship now, and sometimes when one of us notices that the other is upset, we'll smile and say, "Write it on a paper cup."

*The most precious gift
that one person can bestow upon another
is gentle encouragement.*

AUTHOR UNKNOWN

Three Letters from Teddy

ELIZABETH SILANCE BALLARD

Teddy's letter came today and now that I've read it, I will place it in my cedar chest with the other things that are important to my life.

"I wanted you to be the first to know."

I smiled as I read the words he had written, and my heart swelled with a pride that I had no right to feel.

I have not seen Teddy Stallard since he was a student in my fifth grade class fifteen years ago. It was early in my career, and I had only been teaching for two years.

From the first day he stepped into my classroom, I disliked Teddy. Teachers (although everyone knows differently) are not supposed to have favorites in a class, but most especially are they not to show dislike for a child, any child.

Nevertheless, every year there are one or two children that one cannot help but be attached to, for teachers are human, and it is human nature to like bright, pretty, intelligent people, whether they are ten years old or twenty-five. And sometimes, not too often, fortunately, there will be one or two students to whom the teacher just can't seem to relate.

I had thought myself quite capable of handling my personal feelings along that line until Teddy walked into my life. There wasn't a child I particularly liked that year, but Teddy was most assuredly the one I disliked.

He was dirty. Not just occasionally, but all the time. His hair hung low over his ears, and he actually had to hold it out of his eyes as he wrote papers in class. (And this was before it was fashionable to do so!) Too, he had a peculiar odor about him which I could never identify.

His physical faults were many, and his intellect left a lot to be desired, also. By the end of the first week I knew he was hopelessly behind the others. Not only was he behind; he was just plain slow! I began to withdraw from him immediately.

Any teacher will tell you that it's more of a pleasure to teach a bright child. It is definitely more rewarding for one's ego. But any teacher worth her credentials can channel work to the bright child, keeping him challenged and learning, while she puts her major effort on the slower ones. Any teacher can do this. Most teachers do it, but I didn't, not that year.

In fact, I concentrated on my best students and let the others follow along as best they could. Ashamed as I am to admit it, I took perverse pleasure in using my red pen; and each time I came to Teddy's paper, the cross marks (and there were many) were always a little larger and a little redder than necessary.

"Poor work!" I would write with a flourish.

While I did not actually ridicule the boy, my attitude was obviously quite apparent to the class, for he quickly became the class "goat," the outcast: the unlovable and the unloved.

He knew I didn't like him, but he didn't know why. Nor did I know—then or now—why I felt such an intense dislike for him. All I know is that he was a little boy no one cared about, and I made no effort on his behalf.

The days rolled by. We made it through the Fall Festival and the Thanksgiving holidays, and I continued marking happily with my red pen.

As the Christmas holidays approached, I knew that Teddy would never catch up in time to be promoted to the sixth grade level. He would be a repeater.

To justify myself, I went to his cumulative folder from time to time. He had very low grades for the first four years, but no grade failure. How he had made it, I didn't know. I closed my mind to the personal remarks.

First grade: Teddy shows promise by work and attitude, but has poor home situation. Second grade: Teddy could do better. Mother terminally ill. He receives little help at home. Third grade: Teddy is a pleasant boy. Helpful, but too serious. Slow learner. Mother passed away end of the year. Fourth grade: Very slow, but well behaved. Father shows no interest.

Well, they had passed him four times, but he will certainly repeat fifth grade! *Do him good!* I said to myself.

And then the last day before the holiday arrived. Our little tree on the reading table sported paper and popcorn chains. Many gifts were heaped underneath, waiting for the big moment.

Teachers always get several gifts at Christmas, but mine that year seemed bigger and more elaborate than ever. There was not a student who had not brought me one. Each unwrapping brought squeals of delight, and the proud giver would receive effusive thank-yous.

His gift wasn't the last one I picked up; in fact it was in the middle of the pile. Its wrapping was a brown paper bag, and he had colored Christmas trees and red bells all over it. It was stuck together with masking tape.

"For Miss Thompson, from Teddy" it read.

The group was completely silent and for the first time I felt conspicuous, embarrassed because they all stood watching me unwrap the gift.

As I removed the last bit of masking tape, two items fell to my desk: a gaudy rhinestone bracelet with several stones missing and a small bottle of dime-store cologne—half empty.

I could hear the snickers and whispers, and I wasn't sure I could look at Teddy.

"Isn't this lovely?" I asked, placing the bracelet on my wrist. "Teddy, would you help me fasten it?"

He smiled shyly as he fixed the clasp, and I held up my wrist for all of them to admire.

There were a few hesitant ooh's and ahh's, but as I dabbed the cologne behind my ears, all the little girls lined up for a dab behind their ears.

I continued to open gifts until I reached the bottom of the pile. We ate our refreshments, and the bell rang.

The children filed out with shouts of "See you next year!" and "Merry Christmas!" but Teddy waited at his desk.

When they had all left, he walked up to me, clutching his gift and books to his chest.

"You smell just like my mom," he said softly. "Her bracelet looks real pretty on you too. I'm glad you liked it."

He left quickly. I locked the door, sat down at my desk, and wept, resolving to make up to Teddy what I had deliberately deprived him of—a teacher who cared.

I stayed every afternoon with Teddy from the end of the Christmas holidays until the last day of school. Sometimes we worked together. Sometimes he worked alone while I drew up lesson plans or graded papers.

Slowly but surely he caught up with the rest of the class. In fact, his final averages were among the highest in the class, and although I knew he would be moving out of the state when school was out, I was not worried for him. Teddy had reached a level that would stand him in good stead the following year, no matter where he went. He had enjoyed a measure of success, and as we were taught in our teacher training courses, "Success builds success."

I did not hear from Teddy until seven years later, when his first letter appeared in my mailbox.

> *Dear Miss Thompson,*
>
> *I just wanted you to be the first to know, 1 will be graduating second in my class next month.*
>
> *Very Truly Yours,*
>
> *Teddy Stallard*

I sent him a card of congratulations and a small package, a pen and pencil gift set. I wondered what he would do after graduation.

Four years later, Teddy's second letter came.

> *Dear Miss Thompson,*
>
> *I wanted you to be the first to know. I was just informed that I'll be graduating first in my class. The university has*

not been easy, but I liked it.

    Very Truly Yours,

    Teddy Stallard

I sent him a good pair of sterling silver monogrammed cuff links and a card, so proud of him I could burst!

And now today—Teddy's third letter.

Dear Miss Thompson,

    I wanted you to be the first to know. As of today I am Theodore Stallard, M.D. How about that!!??

    I'm going to be married in July, the 27th, to be exact. I wanted to ask if you could come and sit where Mom would sit if she were here. I have no family there as Dad died last year.

    Very Truly Yours,

    Teddy Stallard

I'm not sure what kind of gift one sends to a doctor on completion of medical school and state boards. Maybe I'll just wait and take a wedding gift, but a note can't wait.

Dear Ted,

    Congratulations! You made it, and you did it yourself!

    In spite of those like me and not because of us, this day has come for you.

    God bless you. I'll be at the wedding with bells on!

You Can Do It!

RICKY BYRDSONG, WITH DAVE AND NETA JACKSON
FROM *COACHING YOUR KIDS IN THE GAME OF LIFE*

remember it like it was yesterday. Tenth grade, Frederick Douglass High School in Atlanta. Tall and gangly, I was pushing my way through the crowded hallway. All of a sudden a big, booming voice pealed like a thunderclap behind me, "Hey, son!"

It was Coach William Lester. He was a big, barrel-chested man, six feet, four inches. Besides being the junior varsity basketball coach, he also had a reputation as the school disciplinarian, so the first thing I thought was, *Uh-oh, somebody's in trouble.* He fixed me with his piercing eyes and bellowed, "Yeah, you, son!"

Weak-kneed, I started walking toward him. Oh, my, what had I done? I stopped in front of him, all six feet five inches of me trembling in my shoes.

"Son!" he said, looking me up and down. "You're too big to be walking these halls and not playing basketball. I'll see you in the gym at 3:30—today."

"But, Coach!" I sputtered. "I've never played basketball. I don't have any basketball clothes or shoes."

"Son! Did you hear what I said? I'll see you at 3:30!" And he walked away.

So I went.

And from that day until now, there's no question in my mind that everything that has happened to me since—becoming a basketball player, then a coach, raising my three kids, writing a book—is a result of that day when Coach called me out and said, "Hey, son! Yes, you!"

Up until that point, I hadn't been a troublemaker, but I was drifting. I had no idea what my goals were or where I was heading.

My mom, like so many parents—especially single, working parents—really didn't have time to think about those things. Her goals were pretty basic: "I don't want Ricky on drugs. I don't want him running with the wrong crowd."

Coach Lester helped me see something bigger out there. I remember when he told me, "You can get a college scholarship."

When I said, "But I don't know how. I don't have it," he said, "Yes, you do. I'm going to show you. I'm going to work with you. You can do it."

And he was right. I knew it the day I set foot on a college campus, scholarship in hand. He believed in me. I couldn't let him down.

Many times since the day I heard that big voice bellow, "Hey, son!" I've thought: If only every kid had a Coach William Lester to believe in him, what a difference it would make.

Where the Angel Kissed Me

TIM HANSEL

FROM *WHAT KIDS NEED MOST IN A DAD*

heard a story some years ago about a teenager who had a very obvious birthmark over much of his face. And yet, it didn't seem to bother him. His self-esteem seemed secure. He related well with the other students and was well liked. He seemed to be in no way self-conscious about his very large birthmark, which was obvious to everyone else.

Finally, someone asked how this could be.

"Are you aware of the fact that you have this large birthmark on your face?"

He replied, "Of course I am."

"Can you tell me, then, why it does not seem to bother you in the slightest?"

The young man smiled and said, "When I was very young, my father started telling me that the birthmark was there for two reasons: one, it was where the angel kissed me; two, the angel had done that so my father could always find me easily in a crowd."

He then continued, "My dad told me this so many times with so much love that as I grew up, I actually began to feel sorry for the other kids who weren't kissed by the angel like I was."

The Reason for My Success

S. S.

FROM *SONS: A FATHER'S LOVE*

There's nothing exciting or exceptional about my father. He's a plain-looking guy, and I guess he's pretty ordinary in every way. He has worked as a carpenter all his life, ever since he dropped out of high school. He doesn't read well, and his handwriting and spelling are pretty terrible. But my father has the biggest heart of any man I've ever known.

He always wanted to be sure that I was able to take care of things, so when I was four years old, he gave me a toolbox and some of his old tools. From that time on, he never fixed anything around the house or in our neighborhood without taking me with him. We put together my Christmas swing set. We repaired the patio furniture. We fixed a lamp for the widow next door.

First, Dad would patiently, carefully explain what he was doing, and then he'd ask me to help him. Sometimes he had to do things over two or three times, but he never got mad or frustrated. He seemed to know that I would eventually learn. And little by little, I did.

He did the same thing with our pickup. First, he showed me how he checked the oil, then he taught me how to check the oil myself. He explained how to measure the air in the tires, and before long I was checking the air and water by myself. By the time I was twelve years old, I could change the oil and lube the engine without help.

One day when I was fourteen, Dad and I were driving down a country road on our way to my grandma's house. All of a sudden, Dad pulled the truck over to the side and handed me the keys. "It's time for you to learn to drive, son."

I was both excited and scared. I climbed into the driver's seat, put the key in the ignition, and turned it. I'd always watched Dad shift gears, so I thought I knew what to do, but it wasn't as easy as it looked. I stalled the engine three times, finally got rolling, ground the gears into second and third, and then killed the engine again at a stop sign.

I was all over the road, because when I tried to think about shifting gears, I forgot to look where I was going. It's probably a good thing no one else was on the road, or we might never have made it. But as nerve-racking as it must have been, Dad never once raised his voice. He never got mad or even ruffled. When we pulled into Grandma's driveway, I somehow remembered to put the clutch in and brake at the same time without crashing into the barn. As we came to a stop, he grinned from ear to ear at me. "I knew you could do it. You're going to be a great driver, son."

I've heard it said that parents are supposed to give their kids two things—roots and wings. My dad did both. He made me feel like a part of him, and I always wanted to be where he was. Yet he prepared me to go out into the world by giving me the skills he thought I needed to be a useful and successful man. Today I own my own construction company, and it is named after my dad. He is the reason for my success.

A Day Hemmed in Love

NANCY JO SULLIVAN
FROM *MOMENTS OF GRACE*

I pulled on a string that lit a fluorescent ceiling light and stood looking around my grandmother's basement workshop. Making my way past a worktable laden with scissors and spools, I sat down at her cast-iron sewing machine. Above the machine, a wall plaque read: A Day Hemmed in Love Rarely Unravels.

It had been a month since my grandmother Mema's death. In her last moments of life, Mema had wrapped her hand around mine. Though cancer was invading her bones, her brown eyes bore a beautiful sheen, polished from years of smiling.

"Come back for the sewing machine...it's yours," she had said.

Now, as I opened the bottom drawer of the sewing machine cabinet, I found a collection of fabric swatches, saved patches from treasures that Mema had once sewn for my family.

Although there were piles of gingham and wool and lace squares, a piece of green floral voile caught my eye. As I took the patch into my hand, I forgot that I was a wife and mother of three; now I was seventeen years old, and it was the morning of my senior prom.

Clomping down the stairs that led to Mema's sewing room, my face streaming with exaggerated teenage tears, I plopped my gown on her worktable.

"It looks awful," I wailed.

Mema put on her bifocals, carefully examining the formal I had sewn. The hem was crooked. The waistline was puckering. Threads hung from uneven seams.

Mema shook her head when she saw that I had lined the sheer green flowered bodice with bright yellow satin.

"There wasn't any green lining left; I didn't think the yellow would show through," I whimpered.

"All it needs is the loving touch," Mema said as she held a tape measure to a mismatched sleeve.

For the rest of the day, Mema and I worked side by side at her sewing machine, her shoe tapping the foot pedal as a spool of thread whirled and a needle stitched in a buzz of rhythm.

As Mema mended raveling seams, she reminisced about her past, the hard times of the Depression, losing the farm, the war.

"I sewed your mom's clothes," Mema remembered.

As I handed her pins, I nodded, but I had heard all the stories before.

Preoccupied with the present, I began to chatter on and on about my date for the prom.

"I think he likes me more than I like him," I admitted.

"Maybe the dress will scare him off," Mema joked. We laughed.

When at last the final seams of the formal were sewn, Mema held the dress up to my shoulders.

"Try it on." She looked hopeful, her brown eyes twinkling.

As I donned the refashioned gown, I danced my way past her sewing machine, my hand grazing the back of my hair like a runway fashion model. Though the yellow lining still didn't quite go with the sheer green florals, Mema's impeccable sewing had transformed my dress into a fashion statement.

"You look beautiful." Mema grinned, her aging face a sweet, unforgettable mixture of crow's-feet and smile wrinkles.

"Love you," I said as I kissed her good-bye and rushed home to get ready for the dance.

That night, my date came to the door with a huge, bright pink corsage. He didn't mind that the flowers didn't match my yellow and green gown, he just kept saying how beautiful I looked.

I laughed to myself as I remembered Mema's words, "Maybe the dress will scare him off." As we drove to the prom in an expensive limousine, I got up the nerve to tell him I just wanted to be friends.

"That's okay, let's just have fun," he said.

At the dance we mingled with other teenage friends dressed in tuxedos and gowns. We laughed and danced and ate fancy hors d'oeuvres. Everyone told me how funky my dress looked.

Though it was a memorable night, I can't seem to remember what color tux my date wore or where we went to dinner or even where the prom was held. What I do remember about prom day was the special time I spent with Mema. She had given me a memory to tuck away in my heart for a lifetime, like a precious patch of fabric saved for years in a drawer. I would never forget the laughter we shared, the stories I heard, or the age-old wisdom that had rescued me from certain dress disaster. Her presence in my young life was a thread of love that would never be broken.

I slipped the prom dress patch into my pocket and lifted the sewing machine from the cabinet, carefully placing it into a case I could carry.

I took one last look around Mema's workshop. I wanted to remember the way it looked: the scissors, the spools, and the plaque on the wall.

I wanted to remember A Day Hemmed in Love Rarely Unravels.

Your Gift

Use what talents you possess—
the woods would be very silent
if no birds sang there
except those that sang best.

HENRY VAN DYKE

To Gilbert

CAROL WALKER MARDIROSSIAN

Gilbert was the worst student that crossed my path that first day of school. He came in with no book, pencil, or even paper. He slept through the first thirty minutes until finally I stood directly over him to keep him awake. After class, I kept him for a motivational speech. It was to be one of many with this unruly youngster. After my verbal lashing, he simply said, "Miss Walker, I like you fine. It's just that English ain't never been my thing. I think it's boring and a waste of time. I figure it's a good chance to get a nap before gym. I need my rest to play good."

Shaking my head, I searched for something inspiring to say. Poetic, inspirational messages danced in my head, and then finally I said, "Well, Gilbert. I'll give you a good reason to pay attention in my class. You're never going to graduate if you don't, and I'm going to write you up every day that you breathe hard." I exhaled and grabbed my throbbing head.

Day in and day out for the entire first semester Gilbert came in and enjoyed his rest before gym class. I did as I promised and wrote him up every now and then, to no avail. I gave him extra homework that he didn't do and kept him for detentions. Of course he never showed up. I even wrote his name on the board followed by a long succession of checks. Nothing seemed to work with him.

One day the light came on. I decided that we would have a class spelling bee. My department head had originally asked me to choose the best spellers from my college prep class to participate in the school spelling bee. It was assumed that no one from Gilbert's class would even be in the running. I thought, however, that they should all enjoy the chance. Something magical happened as Gilbert continually spelled words correctly throughout the entire proceeding. It finally came down to the smartest and prettiest little girl in the room and Gilbert, standing there in his faded jeans and ragged T-shirt. I called out the most difficult word of the contest yet, and the little girl answered incorrectly. I looked at Gilbert and he looked at me with panic. I prayed over and over in my mind, *Please, God, let him get it right.* He started to spell the word. He did so slowly and hesitantly. I couldn't stand it. Finally, the moment came and I pronounced him the winner. The whole class cheered as he strutted across the front of the room.

I told the department head that Gilbert would be in the school spelling bee. She couldn't believe it but accepted the news with grace. Of course, Gilbert didn't win the school spelling bee, but that didn't matter. He was there. His mother came to watch and had even bought him a new suit of clothes to wear for the special occasion. Pictures were taken by his mother; and for the day, Gilbert was someone special. The truth is he was all along.

Gilbert never slept in class again. Instead, he began talking incessantly throughout every lesson that I attempted. Somehow it didn't bother me as much anymore. Every now and then he would complete a homework assignment or actually pass a test. I argued with him at times as if I were a child myself competing for attention. There were days when every nerve I had was worn down by him.

The last day of school came. As the bell rang, all of the children ran from the room including Gilbert. I sighed a huge sigh of relief and sat at my desk for a moment to enjoy the silence. Catching my attention from a glance was a little sheet of notebook paper torn off and folded over. It said on the front, "To Miss Walker."

The inside message simply read, "I have enjoyed being in your room this year. I think I even learned a thing or *too.*"

After a refreshing summer, I returned for another year. I walked into my classroom to get ready for the day and there, already seated, was Gilbert. He said, "I'm gonna be in your class again. I asked the assistant principal if I could and she said yes."

I adorned a fake smile and said, "Oh, that's great." The new year proceeded much like the last with a long string of warnings and detentions, mostly for talking. At least he wasn't sleeping in class.

With each new day our relationship as teacher and student grew into one of mutual respect and friendship. Every time he did something bad he gave me his sly little grin, and I just couldn't bring myself to be harsh with him. Instead, I stayed after school tutoring him and helping him pass my class and his other classes.

Near the end of the year, I became engaged and knew that I was going to be moving to a new town. Gilbert came every day of postplanning to help me pack up all of my belongings to begin another life far away.

He said on our last day together, "You're the greatest teacher I've ever had. I probably won't ever like English again because nobody does it as good as you do." I gave him another one of my motivational speeches, except this time I spoke from my heart. I encouraged him to go on and do great things. I knew he was capable of so much.

Every year since, I began the school year saying to myself, "Well, who is going to be my Gilbert this year?" I would laugh and always go on to meet his replacement.

Eight years after leaving Gilbert's school, I talked to one of the teachers there. My first question was, "What ever happened to Gilbert?"

She began by saying, "Well, he never liked English again, but he did pretty well in school. He had some hard times, though, because he couldn't break himself away from some of his friends that were drinking and doing drugs." After a long pause, she continued and revealed to me that Gilbert had died in a wreck just a few weeks before he could graduate. His pregnant girlfriend was in the car with him, but, fortunately, she and the baby were fine. The child was born and named after him.

The news shook me terribly. I wonder if Gilbert knows that he touched my life more than I touched his. He taught me that even the most unlovable child is worth loving. With such a great age and cultural difference, we had become friends. On my next year of teaching I started a new tradition. Instead of wondering who my next Gilbert would be, I spent those few seconds in prayer before any of the students arrived. I asked God to help me love all of my students and to teach at least one person one thing. I held my hand in the air as if toasting and said aloud, "To Gilbert."

What do we live for,
if it is not to make life less difficult for others.

GEORGE ELIOT

The Last Volleyball Game

MICHAEL DAVID ARNOLD

Soon you will be walking onto the court for what may be your last game. It won't be long before the gym will go black as the last flicker of light goes out, and the sounds of applause and cheers will fall as silent as a cool crisp evening in mid-January. No more early practices or long hot hours in August spent in the gym hoping for any sign of a breeze to make its way through to cool you off. In that moment, when you walk off the court, I will be there waiting for you.

As we wait for you to be introduced, your thoughts turn to the future, mine turn to the past. As you prepare to walk onto the court a young lady, I still see the little girl with her backpack on ready for her first day of kindergarten. Eyes full of wonder and hope for everything that would be ahead of you. You put your little hand in mine, and I took you to school knowing that from that day on I would play a smaller role in your life.

Teachers, coaches, and friends would soon see the smile, hear the giggles, and dry your tears. I watched and prayed that God would bring people into your life that cared about you as much as I did.

I remember you heading off with your mom to a mother–daughter banquet and being just a little jealous. It seems no one ever thought to have a father–daughter banquet. I remember you going to games and watching with anticipation of the day you would be able to play. I often think about the influence they had on your life and if someone watching you tonight is waiting with the same anticipation you had. I recall waiting with butterflies in my stomach to see if you made the junior high team. Then heading out to buy just the right pair of shoes that would make you run faster and jump higher.

That same hand that was once so small and a soft voice snap me back to reality.

"Dad, they are introducing me. It is time to go." Yes, it is time to go. But just one more pause as I look for that little girl in your eyes. There she is. I love you more today than yesterday, and I am so proud just to be your dad.

*Giving a smile to someone
is like saying hello without any words.*

BRIANNA ROSSINI

The Secret

ARTHUR GORDON
FROM *A TOUCH OF WONDER*

There's a question that you ask them when they're obviously on their way to the absolute top of the tree, and so I asked it. "How'd you get started?" I said. "Who or what provided the necessary push?"

She gave me a quizzical look. She wasn't really pretty, but she had a merry sort of face. "That," she said, "is a stock question. But never mind: I can give you an answer. We'll have to go back about fifteen years, though."

"That's all right," I said. "Do we have time?"

"We have about five minutes," she said. "That'll do."

And standing there in the chilly dampness, this is what she told me.

In those days, she lived in the twilight land between childhood and adolescence, and she didn't like it much. She was eight years old; she was awkward as a newborn colt, and when she looked in the mirror—which was as seldom as possible—all she could see was a pair of enormous eyes and a lot of complicated bands on her teeth. She was shy, she was lonely, she was convinced that she was hideous. Her name was Margaret, but everyone called her Maggie.

To make matters worse, she had a sister named Sybil who seemed to be everything she was not. Sybil was sixteen, blonde, and cunningly streamlined. She had decided opinions, and on this particular wintry afternoon she was voicing one of them—loudly. "Oh, Mother," she wailed, "do we have to take Maggie? She's only a *child*. And she can't even skate!"

"The Bancrofts asked her, dear," their mother said. "It won't do you any harm to have her along."

Sybil clutched her honey-colored ponytail. "But Larry is taking me! It's all arranged. He…"

"He can take you both," their mother said in tones that even Sybil recognized as final. "Heavens, it's only an afternoon skating party!"

Sybil gave her sister a baleful glance.

"You needn't worry," said Maggie in a small voice. "I'll sit in the back-seat and not say a word."

He came at three o'clock, tall, lithe, the best athlete in the high school. He was seventeen, but he seemed older; there was a kind of quiet assurance about him. Sybil explained in tragic tones that they would have a passenger. Larry looked at Maggie and smiled a little. "That's all right," he said.

They went down the snowy path to the street, Sybil on Larry's arm, Maggie stumbling along behind like a lost puppy. Sybil opened the rear door for her sister. Larry raised one dark eyebrow, but said nothing.

They drove to the lake where the Bancrofts lived, a sheet of magnificent black ice under the gray December sky. Already twenty or thirty skaters were swooping and spinning, their cries thin and sweet in the frosty air. On the shore a bonfire blazed. There were hamburgers and gallons of hot chocolate.

Larry laced Sybil's skates for her. He offered to lace the pair that Maggie had been given for Christmas, but she refused. She would just sit on a blanket, she said, and watch. No, thanks; she wasn't hungry.

She sat there, small and alone, feeling her fingers and toes grow numb. Out on the ice the skaters circled like bright birds, their runners making rhythmic whirring sounds. Watching them, she felt a longing that was almost like physical pain, a longing to be as graceful as they were, as beautiful—as free.

Larry must have been watching her, for suddenly he left the ice and came over, walking on the tips of his skates. He looked down at her. "How about giving it a try?"

She shook her head, mute and miserable.

"Why not?" he persisted. "It's fun."

"I'm no good at it."

"So what?" He sounded genuinely surprised.

She stared at her mittened hands. "My father says that anything worth doing is worth doing well."

He did not say anything for a moment. Then he knelt, unlaced his skates, slipped on his moccasins. "Come on—let's go."

She looked up at him, startled. "Go? Go where?"

"Over there behind that point of trees. Bring your skates."

"Oh, no," she said. "I couldn't. Sybil..."

"Never mind Sybil." His hand was under her elbow, strong, insistent. Incredibly, she was on her feet, walking beside him through the silver dusk. She said, feebly, "Don't you like Sybil?"

"Sure," he said. "I like her fine. I like you, too."

Around the point was a little cove, frozen, secluded, quiet. "This will do," he said. "Put on your skates."

"But I..."

"Put them on. I'll lace them for you."

He laced hers, then his own. He stepped lightly onto the ice and held out his hand. "Come on, Maggie."

She shook her head, her eyes full of tears. "I can't. I'm afraid..."

He said, gently, "I'll tell you why you're afraid. You're afraid because you're lonely. I know because I was lonely once, just like you. Afraid to try things. Afraid of not doing things well. Afraid of being laughed at. But finally I found out something."

He came back and stood beside her. She stared up at him, puzzled, questioning. It was so quiet that she could hear her heart beating. Around them the sentinel pines stood black and motionless. Above the pines, now, the first star gleamed.

"It's funny," he said. "I couldn't tell this to Sybil. I didn't think I could tell it to anyone. But I can tell it to you. What I found out was very simple. It's that no one is ever really alone. Even when there's no other person around, there still must be—Someone. Someone who made you and therefore cares what happens to you. Someone who will help you if you do the best you can. So you're never alone. You *can't* be alone, no matter what you do. That's the secret of happiness, of doing things well, of everything." He held out his hand again. "Come on, Maggie."

She got to her feet and stood there, wavering. But now his right arm was around her waist, his left hand held hers. "All right, now, just relax. Slide your left foot forward and push with your right. That's it. Now slide the right and push with your left! Fine! Now once more...and again...and again..."

That was the story she told me, in five minutes or less. Then the lights went out in the big arena, the music blared, the spotlight caught her as she left me standing in the runway and flashed across the ice on glittering skates to meet the members of the troupe who came spilling out of the other runway. The crowd roared as the rink became a whirling kaleidoscope of color and rhythm and movement. The Greatest Ice Show on Earth, they called it, and I guess it was.

A few yards away I saw her husband standing in the darkness, watching, as he did every night. I moved up and stood beside him. He gave me a quick smile, but all of his attention was out there on the ice. "She's wonderful, isn't she," he said, and it was a statement, not a question.

I looked at his face, so eager and proud. A reporter isn't supposed to feel much, but somewhere inside of me there was a little unaccustomed glow.

"Both of you are, Larry," I said.

But he wasn't even listening.

The Coolest Dad in the Universe

ANGIE K. WARD-KUCER

He was fifty years old when I was born, and a "Mr. Mom" long before anyone had a name for it. I didn't know why he was home instead of Mom, but I was young and the only one of my friends who had their dad around. I considered myself very lucky.

Dad did so many things for me during my grade-school years. He convinced the school bus driver to pick me up at my house instead of the usual bus stop that was six blocks away. He always had my lunch ready for me when I came home—usually a peanut butter and jelly sandwich that was shaped for the season. My favorite was at Christmas. The sandwiches would be sprinkled with green sugar and cut in the shape of a tree.

As I got a little older and tried to gain my independence, I wanted to move away from those "childish" signs of his love. But he wasn't going to give up. In high school and no longer able to go home for lunch, I began taking my own. Dad would get up a little early and make it for me. I never knew what to expect. The outside of the sack might be covered with his rendering of a mountain scene (it became his trademark) or a heart inscribed with "Dad-n-Angie K.K." in its center. Inside there would be a napkin with that same heart or an "I love you." Many times he would write a joke or a riddle, such as "Why don't they ever call it a momsicle instead of a popsicle?" He always had some silly saying to make me smile and let me know that he loved me.

I used to hide my lunch so no one would see the bag or read the napkin, but that didn't last long. One of my friends saw the napkin one day, grabbed it, and passed it around the lunch room. My face burned with embarrassment. To my astonishment, the next day all my friends were waiting to see the napkin. From the way they acted, I think they all wished they had someone who showed them that kind of love. I was so proud to have him as my father. Throughout the rest of my high school years, I received those napkins, and still have a majority of them.

And still it didn't end. When I left home for college (the last one to leave), I thought the messages would stop. But my friends and I were glad that his gestures continued.

I missed seeing my dad every day after school and so I called him a lot. My phone bills got to be pretty high. It didn't matter what we said; I just wanted to hear his voice. We started a ritual during that first year that stayed with us. After I said good-bye he always said, "Angie?"

"Yes, Dad?" I'd reply.

"I love you."

"I love you, too, Dad."

I began getting letters almost every Friday. The front-desk staff always knew who the letters were from—the return address said "The Hunk." Many times the envelopes were addressed in crayon, and along with the enclosed letters were usually drawings of our cat and dog, stick figures of him and Mom, and if I had been home the weekend before, of me racing around town with friends and using the house as a pit stop. He also had his mountain scene and the heart-encased inscription, Dad-n-Angie K.K.

The mail was delivered every day right before lunch, so I'd have his letters with me when I went to the cafeteria. I realized it was useless to hide them because my roommate was a high school friend who knew about his napkins. Soon it became a Friday afternoon ritual. I would read the letters, and the drawing and envelope would be passed around.

It was during this time that Dad became stricken with cancer. When the letters didn't come on Friday, I knew that he had been sick and wasn't able to write. He used to get up at 4:00 A.M. so he could sit in the quiet house and do his letters. If he missed his Friday delivery, the letters would usually come a day or two later. But they always came. My friends used to call him "Coolest Dad in the Universe." And one day they sent him a card bestowing that title, signed by all of them. I believe he taught all of us about a father's love. I wouldn't be surprised if my friends started sending napkins to their children. He left an impression that would stay with them and inspire them to give their own children their expressions of their love.

Throughout my four years of college, the letters and phone calls came at regular intervals. But then the time came when I decided to go home and be with him because he was growing sicker, and I knew that our time together was limited. Those were the hardest days to go through. To watch this man, who always acted so young, age past his years. In the end he didn't recognize who I was and would call me the name of a relative he hadn't seen in many years. Even though I knew it was due to his illness, it still hurt that he couldn't remember my name.

I was alone with him in his hospital room a couple of days before he died. We held hands and watched TV. As I was getting ready to leave, he said, "Angie?"

"Yes, Dad?"

"I love you."

"I love you, too, Dad."

Forever Friends

A true friend
Looks for blossoms
While watering the heart.

KIMBER ANNIE ENGSTROM

Hey, Thanks!

AUTHOR UNKNOWN
FROM *HEARTPRINTS*

One day, when I was a freshman in high school, I saw a kid from my class walking home from school. His name was Kyle. It looked like he was carrying all of his books. I thought to myself, "Why would anyone bring home all his books on a Friday? He must really be a nerd." I had quite a weekend planned, parties and a football game with my friends tomorrow afternoon, so I shrugged my shoulders and went on. As I was walking, I saw a bunch of kids running toward him. They ran at him, knocking all his books out of his arms, and tripping him so he landed in the dirt.

His glasses went flying, and I saw them land in the grass about ten feet from him. He looked up and I saw this terrible sadness in his eyes. As I handed him his glasses, I said, "Those guys are jerks. They really should get lives."

He looked at me and said, "Hey, thanks!" There was a big smile on his face. It was one of those smiles that showed real gratitude. I helped him pick up his books and asked him where he lived. As it turned out, he lived near me, so I asked him why I had never seen him before. He said he had gone to a private school before now. I would have never hung out with a private school kid before.

We talked all the way home, and I carried his books. He turned out to be a pretty cool kid. I asked him if he wanted to play football on

Saturday with me and my friends. He said yes. We hung out all weekend and the more I got to know Kyle, the more I liked him, and my friends thought the same of him.

Monday morning came and there was Kyle with the huge stack of books again. I stopped him and said, "Boy, you are gonna really build some serious muscles with this pile of books every day!" He just laughed and handed me half the books.

Over the next four years, Kyle and I became best friends. When we were seniors, we began to think about college. Kyle decided on Georgetown, and I was going to Duke. I knew that we would always be friends, that the miles would never be a problem. He was going to be a doctor, and I was going for business on a football scholarship.

Kyle was valedictorian of our class. I teased him all the time about being a nerd. He had to prepare a speech for graduation. I was so glad it wasn't me having to get up there and speak. Graduation day, I saw Kyle. He looked great. He was one of those guys that really found himself during high school. He filled out and actually looked good in glasses. He had more dates than I had, and all the girls loved him. Boy, sometimes I was jealous. Today was one of those days. I could see that he was nervous about his speech. So, I smacked him on the back and said, "Hey, big guy, you'll do great!"

He looked at me with one of those looks (the really grateful one) and smiled. "Thanks," he said.

As he started his speech, he cleared his throat. "Graduation is a time to thank those who helped you make it through those tough years. Your parents, your teachers, your siblings, maybe a coach, but mostly your friends. I am here to tell you that being a friend to someone is the best gift you can give them. I am going to tell you a story."

I just looked at my friend with disbelief as he told the story of the first day we met. He had planned to kill himself over the weekend. He talked of how he had cleaned out his locker so his mom wouldn't have to do it later and was carrying all his stuff home. He looked hard at me and gave me a little smile. "Thankfully, I was saved. My friend saved me from doing the unspeakable." I heard the gasp go through the crowd as this handsome, popular boy told us all about his weakest moment. I saw his mom and dad looking at me and smiling that same grateful smile. Not until that moment did I realize its depth.

A friend is a hope of the heart.

RALPH WALDO EMERSON

Standing by Sara

JANE A. G. KISE

Sara was without a doubt the most obnoxious person in our entire high school class of 547 students. And for two hours every day, I had to stand in line by her during diving practice and listen to her long, monotonous, boring, detailed, pointless stories. There were only six divers so I couldn't escape. She chattered as she climbed up on the board and started again right where she left off as soon as she climbed out of the pool.

And what did she talk about? I can tell you everything about her big sister's new convertible—where they got it, how much it cost to upgrade the speaker system, the custom license plates that read WOW, and how smooth it rode even at ninety miles per hour when her dad stepped on the gas to see what it could do.

I also know all about why what she had was better than what I had. For example, "You only have a TI-30 for physics? Ha—my dad ordered a calculator through the university for me." Or, "I can't believe you still ride that old ten-speed bike. I'd rather walk." Or, "You're actually going to use last year's warm-up suit again?"

But the worst was her constant bragging. I mean, how do you answer comments like, "I've got my back one-and-a-half down after only two practices. I bet I'll get 7's on it in the meet tomorrow—you only got 6's last week, didn't you?" After a meet, I heard more from Sara about my mistakes than from our coach, Steve.

Sara was just as obnoxious to Steve. She'd come up from a dive and say, "How's that for a rip? I don't even need to do it again, do I?"

She was totally oblivious to subtle hints. I couldn't bring myself to tell her to shut up, but anyone but Sara would have let up after our one-word responses or distant stares. Even Steve grumbled about her when she was out of earshot.

The last thing I wanted to do was spend any more time with Sara than the two hours a day on diving boards, but luck was not on my side. On a day off from school, Steve scheduled an extra practice. The other divers and I planned on heading to the mall and a movie afterward. Sarah walked into the locker room just as we were discussing which show to see. "Great idea," she said. "Who's driving?"

I turned around, wishing I could say, "My dad's car only has seat belts for five," but that wasn't true. Instead I managed to get out, "I'll pick you up for practice at nine. What time do you have to be home?"

Sara lived on the most exclusive street in our suburb. The next day, when I finally pulled up at the two-story mansion bearing her address, it was more like 9:05; I was hardly in a hurry, knowing I'd be with her for the next seven hours or so. But she still wasn't ready. Her mother invited me in, then bellowed up the stairs, "Sara, stop fussing about what you'll wear. Nothing will make you look pretty like your sister, so just get down here."

I couldn't believe what I'd just heard. To keep from staring at Sara's mother, I quickly glanced around the expansive living room. An antique oriental screen, original sculptures, finely upholstered furniture, a huge picture of Ashley posed with her violin on the grand piano. No picture of Sara. Seeing my gaze, Sara's mom said, "The piano of course is for Ashley. Sara's level of intelligence didn't get her past Chopsticks."

I shivered at the tone of her voice. The whole ornate house seemed chilly, hostile. Her mother's last remark as we left was, "Stay all day if you can—I could use the peace and quiet."

Walking to the car, Sara said, "How soon will you be dropping me off?"

I saw just the slightest quiver in her chin as she tossed her gym bag in the back seat. I tried to imagine how her mother would greet her again—"Stay out of my sight till dinnertime"? I realized I'd never seen Sara's parents at a swim meet or at any other school function. How would it feel to be so unwanted?

As I started the car I said, "Do you have your calculator along? I have to hit the library before supper to get ready for that physics test. You can join me if you want."

Sara's whole face lit up as she undid her seat belt and said, "Just a sec and I'll go get it."

I knew I had to do a better job of being friendly. I described to Steve and the rest of the team what I'd overheard at her house. He rolled his eyes and said, "No wonder."

From then on, Sara frequently joined our table in the cafeteria. We told her in advance about our plans for going out after meets. I learned to steer her chatter toward stories about her dog or the one TV show we both liked. Every time I was tempted to duck when I saw her coming, my conscience warned me, *Come on, be a bright spot in her lonely, cold life.*

Weeks later, when we both qualified for the state swimming meet, it was actually easy to give her a hug and say, "I can't wait—we'll have so much fun together!" And we actually did!

A Friend Is...

Someone who cares about you,
Someone you can trust,
Someone who cheers you up,
Someone who can make you laugh,
Someone you feel comfortable with,
Someone who will always be there for you.

HEATHER SCHWARZBURG
AGE 16

When Friendship Forgives

SUZANNAH WILLINGHAM

T he back door slammed with a crash that set the kitchen windows rattling.

Angry footfalls stomped up the back stairs, then quieted, followed by the thud of the bedroom door closing with force. Something had gone wrong. I'd expected my door to burst open to the radiant, smiling face of my teenage daughter. As I lay in my bed trying to read, long minutes passed. Finally, curiosity had its way and I padded down the hall to her room. Music blared from the boom box but could not cover the sniffs and sobs from the bathroom. Cautiously I peered around the corner to see my daughter, red-eyed and runny-nosed, furiously brushing her hair into a ponytail high on her head.

"Are you okay?" I probed tentatively, already knowing the answer.

"I'm fine. I just can't talk right now. Maybe later."

I swallowed the multitude of questions that swirled in my mind and retreated to my room. Mulling the possibilities, I waited impatiently for her to come and share the events of the evening. I thought of her excitement earlier when a boy, who until recently had been "just a friend," called to invite her to a football game. Having already asked one of her best girlfriends to come for dinner, she accepted with the condition that the friend be allowed to go with them.

As they piled into the car with the boy's mom as chauffeur, a warning buzzed in my head. Maybe a threesome wasn't such a great idea after all. Anne and Kate had been best friends since second grade but had grown somewhat distant in the previous school year. Differences in courses, extracurricular activities, choice of friends, and a decline in church attendance on Kate's part had strained the relationship they were struggling to maintain. Once inseparable, the present found them often going for long periods without spending time together. The evening had been an effort at recementing the friendship.

Anne at last entered my room. A slightly quivery chin, red-rimmed eyes, and an occasional sniff betrayed her attempt at a stoic countenance. Quietly I encouraged her to tell me what had happened. Her reply was quick and to the point. "She stole Greg from me! How could she do it? She is supposed to be my best friend. She knew I liked him. It was a deliberate attempt to hurt me and it worked. Now they are going out. If she hadn't gone with us, this never would have happened! I was trying to be her friend, and she stabbed me in the back."

Momentarily at a loss for words, I remained quiet, stroking her arm and praying for wisdom. The word "forgiveness" loomed large in my mind. "Anne, I know what happened tonight hurts and I know you are angry. You have reason to be, but you know the struggles in Kate's life. Her family is being ripped apart by divorce. This is a difficult time for her and she really needs a friend. So many times, when people are hurting emotionally or feel insecure, they hurt other people in return. It made Kate feel loved and important to take Greg away from you. It was an effort to boost her self-esteem. I know it will be really hard to do, but could you find it in your heart to forgive her?"

Silence greeted my query, then, "She'll never admit she did anything wrong, and she will never say she is sorry."

"You are probably right, and that is when it is most difficult to forgive. Unforgiveness ruins so many relationships. If you can learn now, as a teen, to extend the gift of forgiveness to someone who hurts you, it will be a lesson that will benefit you for the rest of your life." Anne nodded and left my room without further words.

The next day, Anne told me, "I've talked to Kate. Things are a little better. I'm still mad at her. What she did will change everything about my relationship with Greg and my relationship with her. It's not easy, but I've decided to forgive her. I'm not sure I can really trust her anymore, though."

I gave her a big hug and said, "Trust will come back—it just takes time. I am so proud of you for choosing to forgive."

My Forever Friend

=◎=

KRISTI POWERS

it is a friendship that almost didn't happen...but God in his infinite wisdom knew what I needed in my life—one true friend who knew everything about me, thorns and all, but still invited me to share and grow with her in this thing called life.

Len and Kathy Eisert went to the orphanage that crisp fall day with a slip of paper in their hand to see the baby boys, in the hopes of adding one to their family of three. But instead of a bouncing baby boy, the staff brought down one chubby molasses-eyed girl. Realizing their mistake, they started to take the baby girl back to the nursery. Just before they started climbing the stairs, the dark-haired beauty chose to smile at Len with the biggest, toothless grin in the entire world. Right then and there she captured their hearts. Their immediate response was *"No, we'll take her!"* They knew that baby Rachel, as she was soon to be called, was meant for them and only them. That angelic baby was to become my kindred spirit, my forever friend.

I vividly remember the moment I first met her at the age of four. Rachel's oldest sister and my sister were getting together to play, and as my mom dropped off my sister at their house, there she was, sitting on her swing, the dark-haired beauty in contrast to my fair blond locks. From that moment on we were to be friends...bosom buddies.

One day in junior high we were riding home together from basketball practice, and Rachel's mom and she were talking about Rachel's future in basketball. Rachel had developed a noncancerous tumor on her thigh, which had been giving her quite a lot of pain. As we drove along that winter day, Rachel reached for my hand in the dark. I sat with her as she and her mom talked about the possibility of her giving up basketball. That is the way our friendship has always been and I always hope it will be. When the dark times come, we cling to each other and hang on until the light comes again.

Rachel and I are mostly opposites. Rachel was the one who would be prepared and study hard for the PSAT tests for school. I would be beside her getting bored, circling answers just because I felt like it. Rachel was Clinton High School's class valedictorian, and the first girl in our state renowned basketball program to be on the varsity team as a freshman. She was as intense as a person could possibly be. I, on the other hand, went to school to socialize and have fun and was easygoing in my demeanor and personality. I would often show up late for school throughout our senior year as I had a first hour study hall. I would meet Rachel and the principal in the hallway as I entered the school doors. I would say hi to them both and smile my most engaging smile at the principal. He would just shake his head and smile at his troublesome student. Those antics earned me the class award for Most Tardy, while Rachel received the Most Likely to Succeed award.

After graduation from high school, Rachel already had her life planned out before her; I felt confusion over my future and was scared. The day that high school started the next fall, I heard the bus as it made the usual pass by my house. From there it would rumble down the road past Rachel's house, then turn around and head back past my house again and on to school. I don't ever remember feeling so unsure of myself as I did that day. As I sprawled in my bed the abrupt ring of the phone dragged me from my thoughts. I picked up the receiver and it was Rachel saying, "It sure feels weird to not be on that bus, doesn't it?" It was only one of many uncanny moments we have shared throughout our thirty years of friendship.

I can't remember a crucial or happy moment in my life that Rachel has not been beside me, cheering me on, holding my hand, and pointing me toward Christ. Sometimes even giving me a swift kick in the rear. Our friendship is one that even my husband does not understand. Although we are three hours away from each other, we just know when the other needs something. Somehow God has orchestrated our friendship in a way that we will instinctively know when a phone call or card is needed to let the other know that we are there. One time we even sent the exact same card to each other *on the same day.*

When my father died four years ago, Rachel took time off work and stayed throughout the visitation and funeral the next day. Her eyes were constantly on me and anytime I was sitting alone for an extended period of time I would find her sitting or standing next to me, holding my hand or just listening to me. My biggest tears fell when she reached me in the receiving line. "Rachel would know how I feel," I said to myself. "For she is a sister of my heart and my dad loved her like he loved his own kids." I knew she would feel and share in my pain, and she did.

The only regret I have is that in the last few years Rachel has been there for me much more then I have been there for her. I can't count how many times I have called her crying or hurting and she has *never, ever* given me the feeling that I was bothering her, or that she felt that it was time I got over the things hurting me so deeply. I can only pray that I will be there for her—be that sounding block, confidant, and friend that she has been for me

All these thoughts are in my head and heart as I try in my feeble way to thank Rachel for all that she has been and always will be in my life. My forever friend, if you had not been born and your birth mom had not given you up out of her love; if your mom and dad had not seen you that day and had you not captured their hearts, my life would not have been complete until I had found you. You, Rachel, are my one true friend, my forever friend. I thank you from the bottom of my heart.

I Can't Swim

SARA A. DuBose

As I floundered under the water that late-spring day, two thoughts focused in my mind. First, I was sure I was going to drown. Second, I was sorry for lying to Kenny.

Amazed a hunk like Kenny would agree to take me on our Tri-Hi-Y lake trip, I couldn't tell him I didn't even know how to tread water. Kenny played football and sometimes dated one of our cheerleaders. Besides, who ever heard of a fourteen-year-old who couldn't swim?

Some say your past flashes before you in the seconds or minutes before you die. My experience tells me it's at least partly true. I knew why this lie seemed necessary. The problem started back in the third grade. I was the class runt and felt inferior. Nell, the largest girl in our class, was also the leader. Her favorite phrase for me became, "Banana-nose, big-shot baby." I carried the tainted, singsongy phrase around in my head for several years. By junior high, Nell and I were no longer in constant contact, but her opinion became my opinion. If I wanted friends, I would need to pretend. Sometimes it worked and sometimes it backfired. Now was a backfire time.

Why had Kenny pushed me off the pier? It was normal. Guys did it to girls all the time. He expected me to pop right up, act as if I was fuming mad, and try to do the same to him.

I tried. I beat and kick at the flood over me but only sank further.

How long would it take Kenny to see I wasn't coming up? Maybe he wouldn't see at all. Maybe he just ran back up the slope to help someone with the supplies.

Martha. I did have my best friend on this trip. Maybe by now she was on the pier and would tell Kenny I couldn't swim.

No. This was it! I felt a pounding inside my head and a sudden desire to give up. *God, forgive me,* I prayed. *If this is it...*

I stopped struggling. Something bumped my leg. Now I could feel someone's head, then a neck and one, no, two shoulders. Kenny's shoulders. I grabbed one side and then the other as he pushed upward, and in piggyback fashion, lifted me back into time and to Martha's excited voice.

For what seemed like an hour I gagged and sputtered while two or three classmates stopped to stare, pat me on the back, or ask questions. Kenny and Martha stayed with me until I began to come around.

"Why did you tell me you could swim?" Kenny asked. His voice sounded concerned instead of angry.

"I didn't know what you or the others would think. Nobody at my age wants to say, 'I can't swim.'"

"Sara, there's nothing wrong with those two words, 'I can't.' Everyone has something he can't do. Better to accept and admit it than have something drastic happen."

"I know you're right, but...Kenny, I'm sorry I lied to you."

"It's okay. I forgive you. Tell you what. When you're ready, I'll teach you how to swim. Until then, remember. When you can turn an 'I can't' into an 'I can,' do it. When you can't, don't try. Just accept it. When you do, other people will accept you, too. Truth always wins."

I did remember what Kenny said. I thought about it when Martha and I splashed around on the floats talking about boys and our summer plans. I thought about it during the picnic as we began to mingle with the others. I thought about it riding home on the bus while Kenny held my hand. I've thought about it and had it work for me over the years: as a teenager, a collegiate, and on into adult life. Sometimes I wish I could thank Kenny for his sixteen-year-old wisdom.

"When you can turn an 'I can't' into an 'I can,' do it. When you can't, don't try. Just accept it. When you do, other people will accept you, too. They may accept you more. Truth always wins."

Many people will walk in and out of your life, but only true friends will leave footprints on your heart.

ELEANOR ROOSEVELT

True Friends

If you love someone
you will be loyal to him no matter what the cost.
You will always believe in him,
always expect the best of him,
and always stand your ground in defending him.

1 CORINTHIANS 13:7
THE LIVING BIBLE

Darcy's Decision

TERESA CLEARY

Darcy Holmes lay on her stomach and stared at her algebra book while her feet did a midair tap dance to the radio. She wasn't sure if it was the music or the steady drone of her friend Charlotte's voice from across the room that prevented her from concentrating. She'd been looking at the same problem for ten minutes.

Why couldn't I have finished this in study hall like Charlotte did? Darcy asked herself.

She studied her friend from over the top of her algebra book—curly red hair pulled back in a headband, braces, and freckles galore. But Charlotte's eyes were the first thing you noticed about her. They were as green as emeralds, and they could sparkle like the sun or darken with anger or tears. They were the kind of eyes that were hard to look into and tell a lie—but lying to Charlotte was exactly what Darcy was thinking about.

After all, I have a right to make new friends besides ones from church, don't I? Darcy asked herself. *I don't have to go to every youth group party, do I? How am I ever going to be popular at school if I don't make an effort?*

And so Darcy was considering skipping this weekend's youth group overnighter to go to a party with her friend, Lisa—one of the most popular girls at school. She was even considering lying to her parents and saying she was going on the overnighter and instead staying at Lisa's. The only problem was she wasn't sure how she'd pull it off.

Darcy threw down her pencil. *What should I do?* She wondered.

"Darcy!" Charlotte's voice interrupted. "You're not listening."

"Sorry. I have a lot on my mind," Darcy admitted.

"Got enough problems of your own that you don't want to hear other people's, right?" Charlotte said with a laugh.

Darcy felt like Charlotte had read her mind, until she realized her friend was talking about the algebra homework.

Darcy shut her book and sat up on the bed. "What's up?"

"Well, my problem is there's this girl I know who's really nice, but all of a sudden she wants to be part of the in crowd at school. That never used to matter to her, but now—well—it's all she thinks about."

Darcy was having a hard time meeting Charlotte's eyes. She could relate perfectly well to how this girl felt.

"I think this girl may do something dumb this weekend like give up a great overnighter at church to go to a party where there's sure to be drinking and stuff. I don't think she should go, but I'm not sure how to tell her. What do you think?" Charlotte asked a little too innocently.

As Darcy realized Charlotte already knew all about her plan, her temper flared. She knew her friend was trying to look out for her, but this was too much.

"I think you should just butt out and let this girl do what she wants," Darcy retorted. "She's a big girl."

"But is she a smart girl?" Charlotte flung back.

"I can make my own decisions," Darcy said.

"Can you?" Charlotte asked. "Like when we were kids and you decided you'd be cuter with short hair, so you cut all your hair off about two inches from your head. Then you looked so bad you tried to convince me to do it so at least you wouldn't be miserable alone. Great decision, Darcy."

Darcy couldn't help but smile. It had taken years for her hair to grow back in. "Okay, that was a bad decision, but I was only seven."

"Well, you're fifteen now, and you're about to make another bad decision. A major one. I think you should reconsider your priorities."

When Charlotte left later, Darcy called Lisa. "What time will the party start?" she asked.

"Right after the game," Lisa replied. "But we'll let things get going before we arrive."

"Will there be beer?"

"Of course. Troy's brother got a keg."

"I guess his parents aren't going to be around."

"Are you crazy? They left town for a trip to Hawaii. Troy and Geoff are on their own. Hey, you aren't getting cold feet, are you?" Lisa asked.

"I—I have to go, my mom's calling me," Darcy said, glad to get off the phone. "I'll call you later."

When she hung up, Darcy was more confused than ever. As much as she wanted to be part of the in crowd, she wasn't sure this was the way to do it. But then again, it might be her only chance.

"Darcy, time for dinner!" her mom called again.

After dinner Darcy headed back to her room. Almost immediately the phone rang.

"Darcy, it's for you," her mom called.

"Darcy, it's Pam. I'm in charge of refreshments for this weekend. Can you bring a bottle of pop and a bag of chips? It would help a lot."

"Uh, I'm not sure if I'm going, Pam. Can I let you know?"

Darcy was back in her room when the phone rang again. It was Jill calling to say she hoped Darcy would make the overnighter. Jill's phone call was followed by one from David, then Ellen, then Scott, then Luke, then Terri.

When Darcy hung up with Terri, the doorbell rang. She heard Charlotte's voice as her dad let her in. "I came to talk to Darcy."

Darcy walked out into the hallway and crossed her arms.

"Did anyone call?" Charlotte asked innocently.

Darcy couldn't help it. She burst out laughing. "Yes, someone called. Someone named Pam, and David, and Ellen, and Scott, and Luke, and Terri. Should I expect any more pressure to sway my decision?"

"Well, there won't be any more calls," Charlotte said, her green eyes dark. "Just a visit—from a friend who wants to see you do the right thing."

"You really outdid yourself," Darcy said. "Did you ask everyone from youth group to call?"

"Just the ones who care," Charlotte replied.

"That's a pretty convincing argument," Darcy said quietly.

"Darcy, I don't know why being popular is such a big thing with you lately, but I wanted you to see how popular you already are. Maybe it is with youth group and not with the crowd at school, but we all really care about you. I know we're pressuring you to go with us this weekend, but I didn't know what else to do. I felt like since Lisa and her friends were pulling you in one direction, I needed to start pulling you in the other."

"A tug-of-war, huh?" Darcy asked.

"Kind of," Charlotte admitted.

"Well," Darcy said, looking into Charlotte's eyes, "call it a victory. Your side won."

"Great!" Charlotte said, pulling Darcy toward the phone. "C'mon, you have a lot of calls to return."

Darcy looked at her friend and smiled. She was glad to see the sparkle back in Charlotte's green eyes.

Imagination Highway

SARAH McGHEHEY
AGE 18

Remember a summer you had that was just plain fun? One where you can still hear the laughter echoing through your ears, feel the Kool-Aid soothing your throat, and look down and see your dirty feet while you long to run inside the house and eat the turkey sandwich your best friend's mom made for you? Those were the days.

I have a friend named Mandy. We have been friends for eight years, and even at eighteen, I can still say "thanks" to her for teaching me the meaning of true friendship and genuine fun.

As kids, Mandy and I were "outdoor" girls—into building forts, swimming in ponds, running through the woods, and riding four-wheelers. Why stay inside playing with dolls when there was a world to conquer outside?

One particular sunny summer day stands out in my sea of memories. We were visiting her neighbor, Stephen, and he was three years older than us. We thought he was really cool, and that we were even cooler—just because we could hang out with him.

That day we were in the midst of an intense two-on-one basketball game when Mandy's mom called us home for dinner. We said our good-byes, and after Stephen went inside, the fun started. Mandy and I looked at each other, then down his long, steep gravel driveway, then our eyes met again; we knew what this meant…

You see, we had these imaginary worlds that we would travel to together—as if our minds were connected.

This time we were both drivers behind the wheels of expensive sports cars with no shocks. So we started to bounce as we walked, our feet shuffling in the slippery, bumpy gravel. We bobbed our heads, held onto our imaginary steering wheels, and pretended as if we were somewhere in the uncivilized wild of Africa, on the roughest terrain, trying to find the right path for our sports cars. We made "uh, uh, uh" noises, just like the kind you make when you hum and someone pounds on your back at the same time. We bumped and jolted along, laughing the whole way down toward the bottom, picking up speed as we went.

I was beginning to feel a little dizzy, but I kept going. I looked beside me and Mandy was gone; I whirled around. She was face first in the gravel. *What happened?* I panicked. She was crying hysterically and was scraped up, face and all. I ran to get her dad, but I couldn't exactly explain to him what had happened (you can see why).

She recovered after a little washing up and a couple of faithful Lion King Band-Aids.

This story probably made you laugh, as we did—after the incident. But that's not the entire point of it. Through experiences such as this, I have learned the joy of the gift of imagination when shared with a friend. It is a great blessing; it can bring the most heartfelt joy, join your kindred spirits, and spring forth laughter. Get away on the imagination highway with your friends; it's the best road to take. Just be sure it's not gravel.…

Dance Lessons

JANE A. G. KISE

As the last few seconds of the homecoming football game ticked away, I stuffed my French horn into its case as quickly as I could and looked around for Dale, my date for the dance. I still couldn't believe that the top musician, track star, and president of our class had asked me. But where was he now? I scanned the other bleacher sections and spotted him hurrying down the steps on the far side. I waved and he called, "You'll still be ready in a half hour?"

I nodded, but I wanted to answer, "I've been ready for two years. From the day we met as ninth-grade science lab partners." We were both in the same crowd from band, so I'd been sledding with him, to movies and parties, on skit and float committees; but I was just one of a dozen girls he considered his friends.

At the start of our junior year, though, Dale and I ended up sitting together in the orchestra pit for a musical. And we were assigned to do a joint history project. A few study sessions later, he asked me to homecoming. *Me!* For four weeks, we'd walked between classes together, walked home together...the whole school knew we were dating.

The evening unfolded just as I'd dreamed. Dale arrived right on time to pick me up, and we headed to a great seafood restaurant. He grinned as we sat down and said, "Let me order tonight."

By candlelight, we dined on crab cakes, chowder, lobster. I tried to wave aside dessert, but Dale said, "You have to try one of their tortes. We'll share."

Trading bites and laughing as we swapped school stories, I kept thinking what a great year it was going to be at Dale's side for band trips, Snow Dance, prom. Sadie Hawkins, the girl-ask-boy dance, was just a few weeks away. I put down my fork and said, "So, what are you doing on the twenty-first?"

Dale looked blankly at me. "For what?"

"Sadie Hawkins. You'll go with me?"

"Uhh...Myra already asked me."

I almost choked. Myra was a good friend of mine. She must have asked him at the football game when he disappeared toward the end. Come to think of it, they'd talked after band all week. What an idiot I'd been! Dale probably wished he was with Myra right now. I managed to mumble, "I hope you two have a good time," as I chased a chocolate crumb across my plate.

The waiter brought our check. I stared at my napkin, thinking, *God, how can this be happening? How can I show my face at school again?*

Then Dale made the strangest sound. When I looked up, Dale's face had taken on the greenish tint of our school cafeteria walls. "What's wrong?" I asked.

Dale stood up, checking his pockets. "My wallet. I must have left it at home."

Revenge. And I hadn't had to do anything. Oh, how I'd enjoy watching Dale try to explain this to the manager. After all, the whole band probably knew by now that he'd been with Myra at the game.

But a voice inside me said, *And you call yourself a Christian?* I had enough emergency money from my father to cover the bill. I knew the voice was right. I pulled the wad of bills out of my purse and let Dale pay the waiter.

But I didn't have enough cash left to get us into the dance. I wondered about calling it quits on the evening, but I knew it would be easier to talk to my friends Monday if I at least appeared at the dance. We drove to his house in silence.

Dale took me inside and introduced me to his parents. His dad said, "Why aren't you at the dance already?"

Dale looked at his shoes. "I forgot my wallet."

"You what? Of all the irresponsible, foolish…" His dad went on in that tone for a good five minutes. Dale did his best to melt his six-foot frame into the carpet. Finally, he managed to grab his wallet, and we made a dash for the car.

Once inside, Dale leaned back for a moment and shook his head. At that point I calculated that he and I were about even on the humiliation scale for the evening. I said, "Hey, we could be scraping lobster shells and congealed butter off plates back at the restaurant."

He looked at me, then said, "I've sort of blown this evening for you, haven't I?"

He said it just like any friend would, this guy who had been a good friend for more than two years. And suddenly I knew I still wanted to be friends. And I knew somehow I had to forgive him—and Myra, too. I said, "Well, we'll still get there in time, unless you manage a flat tire or something."

He laughed as he started the car, saying, "At least I know the gas tank is full."

By the time we got to the dance, we were back where we started— good friends. I was so cheerful I even told Dale to take a few dances with Myra.

Some of my friends couldn't believe that I could still study with him. Or that we did skits together at parties. Or that I didn't care who he took to Snow Dance or prom. Maybe it was just a bit of a miracle that his forgotten wallet urged me into forgiving him right then and there.

Getting It Right

MOLLY NOBLE BULL

It rained on the April morning I found out about Lucy's mother—a light, cooling sprinkle of tears that grayed the Texas sky. I didn't know what kind of cancer Mrs. Hastings had until later, but I knew her condition was serious—very serious.

Now don't get me wrong. I love Mr. and Mrs. Hastings almost as much as I love my own parents, and Lucy is my best friend. But I didn't want to go to school that day. And I sure didn't want to see Lucy.

What could I possibly say to her? What do people say to their friends at such a time? I was afraid to send Mrs. Hastings so much as a get-well card because I wasn't sure she was going to get well. I tried every trick I knew to get out of going to school. But Mom insisted.

"You have a history test this morning, Kristin," she said, looking at me as if she'd crawled into my mind and knew I was just making excuses. "Had you forgotten?"

"No, Mother, I hadn't forgotten."

She smiled. "Be sure to stay close to Lucy, especially today, because that poor girl is going to need your strength."

Strength? What was Mother talking about? I had no strength. I didn't even know what to say to my best friend.

I hid out in the choir room between classes in hopes of avoiding Lucy, but she was never out of my thoughts. I kept trying to come up with something appropriate to say to her because I really wanted to get it right. Why, I even wrote out a dialogue, stating what I would say and what she would say. But in the end, I tore up the paper because it simply didn't sound like me.

Lucy and I had last period English in Mrs. Green's room. Though I'd eluded her all day, I was going to have to face her last period, and I still didn't have a plan. However, I worried needlessly because Lucy never showed up for class.

When English class was over, Mrs. Green said, "Kristin, I know Lucy Hastings is your best friend, and I would like to know how she is handling her mother's illness."

"I don't know how she's handling anything," I said, "because I haven't seen or heard from Lucy since yesterday."

"Well, you'll be seeing her shortly because Lucy is coming here to my room in a few minutes to get her lesson assignments."

"Lucy is coming here?"

Mrs. Green nodded, and my heart pulled into a hard knot; I began to tremble inwardly. I still didn't know what to say to her, and time was running out.

"Excuse me, Mrs. Green," I finally said, "but I have to—to go now." I bolted the classroom, fast.

I raced down the hall and out the front door of school practically in one breath. Then I joined the students who were headed for the campus parking lot.

It had stopped raining, and the air smelled clean and fresh. A rainbow cut across a sky still darkened by thunderclouds, and the wind tossed my hair in all directions—until I pulled up the hood of my yellow raincoat.

In the distance I saw someone coming toward me. Somehow, I knew it was Lucy.

She had her head down, and she was wearing a yellow raincoat exactly like mine. She'd pulled her hood up too; maybe she hadn't seen me. Maybe if I ran back inside and hid in the choir room again, she wouldn't find me.

Then I noticed how Lucy's shoulders shook with every step she took. And I knew she must be crying because I was.

The rain came down again. Raindrops mingled with my tears. Lucy's heart was breaking, and I wasn't doing a thing to help her.

As I grew closer, my throat tightened, making it impossible to speak even if I'd known what to say, and a deep ache filled my heart. I prayed for strength, strength my mother claimed I already had, and I forced myself to move forward, arms outstretched.

"Oh, Kristin," Lucy shouted. "I was hoping it was you."

We hugged then, but I still couldn't utter a sound.

Looking back, I learned something that day that I might never have grasped in any other way. You see, I'd been focusing on me, Kristin Rogers. What should I do? How should I act? What will I say to Lucy?

But when we finally came face to face, I forgot me and centered on Lucy and her needs. When I did that, I was able share Lucy's grief—let her know that she was special and that I really cared.

Since then, Lucy has told everyone she sees that I have the gift of saying just the right words at just the right time. I still don't think she realizes that on the day we hugged in the April rain, I never said a word.

I've dreamed of meeting her all my life...a bosom friend—an intimate friend, you know—a really kindred spirit to whom I can confide my inmost soul.

L. M. MONTGOMERY
FROM *ANNE OF GREEN GABLES*

The Invisible Signs

STEVE LAWHEAD

There is an invisible sign in the middle of the cafeteria. It reads: Territory of the Senior Class Socialites—All Others Keep Out! Although the sign is invisible, everyone can read it. Everyone knows and obeys. There are other posted territories: the far end of the student concourse, near the drinking fountain, the grassy hill in front of the school entrance. No trespassing! Keep out! This area belongs to us!

Belonging. That's what those invisible signs mean. To those on the inside they form the boundaries of a refuge, an island of safety in a sea of self-consciousness.

My group has staked out the lunchroom. From the security of our island in the middle of the lunchroom, I sometimes feel guilty as I look out at the loners. They sit alone, eat alone. Or they slouch behind their books and act like they're studying.

But they're not studying; they're watching us. Their eyes betray them. I've seen the looks of unguarded envy they throw our way. They are saying, "If only I could join the group..." But it's impossible—there are unwritten rules governing these things.

I can only imagine what the outsiders are feeling. Yet some days there is a split second of uncertainty just before I reach my group. I wonder, *What if they don't recognize me? What if they don't let me in?* But I approach and the ranks open to admit me. I slap my tray down and I'm in—safe inside for another day.

I have learned to play the games you have to play to fit in. I know all the moves, the rules, and the talk. I wear the mask the group wears and never, never let anyone see the real me. There's security there. I'm in. I belong. As long as I go along with the group—do as they do, act as they act, think as they think. Those are the rules. Break them and you're out. Then you'll be a loner holding your tray and looking for a place to sit. On the outside looking in.

I sometimes argue with the guilt: *Is it my fault for enjoying what everyone wants? What am I supposed to do? Quit? If I quit the group, what good would that do? Who would that help? Could I just walk away and be myself?* Deep inside I know the answers. Deep inside I must admit the truth: I *need* the clique. I'm too afraid to stand alone, to be myself. My fear keeps me tied to the group.

Still, I'm haunted by the eyes of the outsiders. They're always watching. I used to think they could tell I was different, that even though I ran with the group I still had my own identity. Now, I'm not so sure. Last week I saw a kid in the library—one of those who sits alone at lunch and studies while we're all cutting up. We were looking for the same book, he and I. We saw it at the same instant and reached for it. I got there first. I looked at his eyes behind the thick glasses and felt a little sorry for him. I wanted to do a friendly thing so I offered the book to him. He looked at it, then at me, and turned his back. As he walked away I heard him mumbling to himself. The others said the kid was a stuck-up snob when I told them. Funny, that's what he'd muttered about me.

Why do we have these cliques? Why can't we all just be ourselves? Unself-conscious. Not pretending to be the laughing, careless, and cool people we're not. I wonder, what is everyone afraid of? If I decided to take one lunch hour and sit with a loner, what would happen? What if we all did that? There'd be a revolution—a quiet revolution. And a lot of people would be freed that day. But I don't look for anything like that to happen. It's just too hard.

A choice must be made. I can see that now. It would be better if one or two of my friends in the group saw that, too. Maybe they do. Maybe they feel the same way I feel—trapped, stuck in the clique, but afraid to leave. Maybe they're waiting for someone to break free, to step out and risk something new.

There's one good way to find out.

The Swing

TERESA CLEARY

aura, Jenny, and I sat rocking on the swing on Laura's front porch. Since Jenny had the longest legs, it was her job to keep us moving with a gentle push every now and then. Today our swinging was sporadic. Jenny was caught up in Laura's description of the heart surgery she would undergo in two days.

"The doctors say now is the best time," Laura explained. "I've grown all I'm going to, I'm healthy, and they don't want to wait any longer. The walls of my aorta are weakening every day."

Jenny and I listened quietly. We'd always known that one day Laura would have heart surgery, but we weren't prepared for it to happen this summer. We were having too much fun.

Jenny and I had always known Laura was different. She often complained about the way her eyes protruded from her head and about the extra-thick glasses she wore. We teased her about her slightly bucked front teeth and lovingly called her "Bugs" after Bugs Bunny. But we never teased her about her heart condition. Laura's family had known from her birth that one day she would require an operation. Now the day had come.

Laura went shopping with her mom the next day, so Jenny and I didn't see her until late. We sat on the porch swing, each of us lost in our own thoughts. When Laura's dad called her in, I hugged her tightly. "I'll be praying for you," I said.

"Thanks," she replied with a smile. "Pray for the doctors, too." We all laughed. Laura's remark had broken the tension.

I didn't sleep very well that night, so it was late when I got up the next morning. I went outside for some fresh air and looked down the row of houses to Laura's. I saw her dad and brother with their arms around each other.

They're home early, I thought. I went in the house just as the phone rang. It was Jenny.

"Teresa, I have terrible news."

I could tell she was crying. My heart sank.

"Laura died," Jenny said flatly. "When the doctors touched her aorta, it was so weakened it just dissolved. She died on the operating table."

I was in shock. "Jenny, I'll talk to you later," I said and hung up the phone. As I headed for my room, I passed my mom in the hall.

"Any news on Laura?" she asked.

I shook my head, still too stunned to tell anyone the news I didn't want to believe. I shut my door and lay down on my bed.

It can't be true, I told myself. *Laura can't be dead. Jenny heard wrong. It was some other girl who died. Laura will call and tell me everything's okay.*

As the hours stretched on, I knew Jenny was right—but I couldn't admit it. I heard Jenny's mom call mine to tell her the news. When my mom knocked on my door, I told her to go away. "I want to be alone."

On the way to the funeral home, I kept telling myself that Laura was okay. But when I walked into the room with my parents and saw Laura lying there, reality hit. My friend was dead. I walked over to the casket and looked at Laura's peaceful face. She looked like she could jump up any minute and ask why everyone was so sad, but she didn't. Laura was dead.

I cried hot, angry tears. I couldn't understand why Laura had died, and I was mad at God for allowing it to happen. *The world is full of horrible people. Why didn't You take one of them? Why did You have to take the sweetest, kindest person I know?*

God didn't give me any easy answers. At Laura's funeral, her pastor read John 3:16: "For God so loved the world that He gave His only begotten Son, that whoever believes in Him shall not perish, but have eternal life."

I knew Laura was a Christian, and I was comforted by the fact that she was promised eternal life. As the days passed, I drew on God's promises for those who believe in Him. Jesus told His disciples that He was going to prepare a place for them in heaven. 1 knew that included a mansion for Laura. I missed Laura terribly, but I could feel my anger lessening.

One evening several weeks later, Jenny and I were walking when we found ourselves heading for Laura's front porch. We sat on the swing, both uncomfortably aware of the space between us.

"I miss Laura," Jenny said as she gave a push.

"Me too," I replied placing my hand on the empty seat. "But you know," I told Jenny with a smile, "Bugs will have perfect teeth in heaven."

Jenny laughed. "You're right, and she can't complain about her eyes or her thick glasses anymore!"

"And no heart defect..."

The front door opened and Laura's mom came out. "I thought I heard someone," she said. "I was hoping you girls would stop by. Please keep using the porch swing. Laura's dad put it up for the three of you, and we hate to see it empty."

"We'll be back," we promised.

"No heart defect," Jenny said with wonder as our swinging resumed.

We scooted together, closing the space that had separated us. "Do you suppose there are porch swings in heaven?" Jenny asked.

"I'm sure of it," I said firmly. "And I'm sure Laura will be saving us a place on one when we get there."

Love's
All in the Family

Home is a place
That speaks peace to your soul
Holds your heart gently
And welcomes you with love and forgiveness.

JUDY GORDON MORROW

Wrinkle in My Hood

KEN PIERPONT

We live in a very quiet neighborhood.

Late one evening I was listening to some music when I heard a loud crash on the street. It took me a while to realize what had happened.

Earlier that evening my wife wanted me to go to the store to get some soft drinks. It seemed like this would be a good time to let my teenage daughter get in a little practice driving. I sent her to the store with her older brother riding shotgun. She took my truck. I settled back to enjoy the music.

At dinner earlier that evening my oldest son was speaking admiringly of the truck. It is a little four-wheel drive Ford Explorer, and the kids knew I enjoyed having it. It is the nicest car I have ever owned.

I said, "Guys, my heart is not set on that car. I like it, but it is just rusting metal and it is a depreciating item. It won't last forever. Never set your heart on anything that is temporary."

I had no idea how prophetic my advice was that night.

The thud on the street was followed by a commotion upstairs, and then the whole family pouring down the steps led by thirteen-year-old Chuck who shouted, "Dad! Dad! Holly wrecked your car."

My heart sank and my mind was flooded with conflicting thoughts. *Was anyone hurt? Who else was involved?* I ran to the door with a racing heart, and in that instant a message came clearly to my spirit like a voice in my heart:

Here is your chance. You have always looked for ways to show Holly that she is precious to you. Here is a unique opportunity to show her what you really love. How you react now is something that she will probably never forget.

To my surprise the accident had not occurred on the street, but right in my own driveway. And my fears about damage to the property of other people melted when I saw that the collision was with our other car, the family van. In her inexperience Holly had confused the brakes and accelerator. In an instant both of my cars were wrecked. Holly was unhurt physically, but when I reached her she was crying softly and saying over and over again, "Oh, Dad, I'm sorry. I'm sorry, Dad. I know how much you love this car." I wrapped her in my arms, and she cried and my heart melted for her.

Later that week an adult friend stopped by and asked what happened to my truck. I swore her to secrecy and then told her what happened. Her eyes moistened and she said, "That happened to me when I was a girl. I borrowed my dad's car and ran into a log that had fallen across the road. I was able to drive the car home, but it was totaled. When I got home, my dad was so angry he grabbed me and dragged me out of the car. When he exploded with rage, it was obvious the car meant more to him than I did." Over forty years later the pain of that rejection still moved her to tears. It was a deep wound on her soul.

I remembered how tenderhearted Holly had been the night she wrecked the car and how vulnerable she was at that moment, and I breathed a prayer of thanks to God for His gentle reminder that night. Someday years from now when Holly thinks back on her life and she remembers me, I want her to know that I loved her a thousand times more than all my earthly possessions put together.

I repaired the van, but the wrinkle in the hood of my truck is still there today. Every day it reminds me of the really priceless things in my life. I don't mind having damage to my truck, but I don't want to be responsible for damage to my daughter's heart.

Winning Isn't Everything

TIFFANY ADAMS
AGE 17

His hands were balled into fists tighter than wire. The vein in his neck was bulging so large that I could see his pulse. When I looked at his eyes they were dripping with tears of anger and frustration. What he did at that next moment changed my life.

We were in the middle of a soul-shredding fight. We were biting into each other, attacking with our words. My brother and I both had our own secret war tactics that drove each other insane. We were on opposite sides of the room, like two boxers in the ring, flinging our hate-filled words back and forth like punches. If someone had walked into the middle of the fight, he would have thought we were archenemies, not brother and sister, who minutes before had been laughing together.

As the argument grew more and more fierce, we began to throw sharper arrows that would leave deeper scars. At the crescendo of the argument he went silent. In the middle of his sentence he stopped. I paused only for a moment, wondering why he had become silent, but since I was determined to win the war, I ignored it and took it as my cue to go in for the kill. I began to approach him, ready to drive my sword into his heart while keeping my shield up. But as I moved toward him, spewing words that I would soon regret, my gaze met his, and the look that he gave me stopped me so suddenly that I stumbled and went silent.

He looked at me, his eyes full of nothing but love. There stood my brother, my popular, perfect brother, crying for me. He looked at me, shaking with self-control, and said, "Tiffany, I love you."

The armor and sword that moments before I had been ready to kill with, disappeared as I was immersed in shame. I had never before seen my brother cry, yet there he stood shedding tears of restraint, and for me, not because I had hurt him but because he loved me so much and didn't want to fight anymore.

I wanted to tell him I was sorry and eat my words, but I couldn't. It wouldn't matter what I said because nothing could amount to what he had just done. There was no way I could be as mature as he had just been. He had taken simple words that we say every day and made them change my life.

I have never looked at my brother the same since that moment. He showed me kindness and care in a way I had never seen before. The maturity it took for him to say that is more than I will ever have. He suffered to show me love.

When he walked out of that room and left me with my shame, he did, in fact, change my life. Seconds before he uttered those words, winning that argument was everything. I will never again approach an argument intending to hurt or attack. My brother showed me that the person is always more important than the fight.

Filling His Shoes

MELISSA KNAPP

My father died when I was five. It was hard on us all. With time the wounds healed. My brother, who is eight years older than me, began to watch over my mother and me.

Taking on many more responsibilities than was expected of him, I remember he made sure the trash was taken out and the yard mowed. He did it on his own, without being told to do so.

Because of my father's death, my mother was forced to get a full-time job. My brother took it upon himself to get up early every morning. He would get me up for school and make me breakfast. While I was eating he would lay out my clothes, make my bed, and gather my schoolbooks up.

Hand in hand we would walk to the bus stop. As we waited, he would play games my father used to play with me. He did his best to make me happy, and he succeeded every time.

When we arrived home from school, we were alone for about a half hour until Mom was home from work. He would sit me down with three cookies and a glass of milk. If I had homework, then this was the time I would do it. My brother would start laundry and do dishes, if there were any. He would find something for supper and have everything ready for Mom, so she could start cooking.

Mom would greet us with a hug and kiss. That was our cue to go outside and have some fun. It was my brother's time to be a kid.

A Saturday in June a couple of years later, my mother and I were at the store. They had the Father's Day cards out. I stared at the rack of cards. My mom said, "Honey, I know this is a hard time for you."

I said "No, Mom, that's not it. Why don't they have Brother's Day cards?"

She smiled and said, "You're right, your brother has definitely been a father to you. Go ahead, pick out a card."

So I did, and on Father's Day, my mother and I sat my brother down and gave him the card.

As he read it, I saw the tears forming in his eyes. I felt a lump in my throat, as he threw his arms around me and my mother. I heard the crackling in Mom's voice as she said, "Son, your father is proud of you, seeing that he raised a good man, and that you do your best to fill his shoes. We love you, and thank you."

Mother's Legacy

I shall never forget my mother
for it was she who planted and nurtured
the first seeds of good within me.

IMMANUEL KANT

Away in a Manger

TIM MADIGAN

One afternoon about a week before Christmas, my family of four piled into our minivan to run an errand, and this question came from a small voice in the backseat:

"Dad," began my five-year-old son, Patrick, "how come I've never seen you cry?"

Just like that. No preamble. No warning. Surprised, I mumbled something about crying when he wasn't around, but I knew that Patrick had put his young finger on the largest obstacle to my own peace and contentment—the dragon-filled moat separating me from the fullest human expression of joy, sadness, and anger. Simply put, I could not cry.

I am not the only man for whom this is true. We men have been conditioned to believe that stoicism is the embodiment of strength. We have traveled through life with stiff upper lips, secretly dying within.

For most of my adult life I have battled depression. Doctors have said much of my problem is psychological, and they have treated it with medication. But I know that my illness is also attributable to years of swallowing rage, sadness, even joy.

Strange as it seems, in this world where macho is everything, drunkenness and depression are safer ways for men to deal with feelings than tears. I could only hope the same debilitating handicap would not be passed to the next generation.

So the following day when Patrick and I were in the van after play-ing at a park, I thanked him for his curiosity. Tears are a good thing, I told him, for boys and girls alike. Crying is God's way of healing people when they're sad. "I'm glad you can cry whenever you're sad," I said. "Sometimes daddies have a harder time showing how they feel. Someday I hope I do better."

Patrick nodded. In truth I held out little hope. But in the days before Christmas I prayed that somehow I could connect with the dusty core of my own emotions.

"I was wondering if Patrick would sing a verse of 'Away in a Manger' during the service on Christmas Eve?" the church youth director asked in a message left on our answering machine.

My wife, Catherine, and I struggled to contain our excitement. Our son's first solo.

Catherine delicately broached the possibility, reminding Patrick how beautifully he sang, telling him how much fun it would be. Patrick him-self seemed less convinced and frowned. "You know, Mom," he said, "sometimes when I have to do something important, I get kind of scared."

Grown-ups feel that way too, he was assured, but the decision was left to him. His deliberation took only a few minutes.

"Okay," Patrick said. "I'll do it."

From the time he was an infant, Patrick has enjoyed an unusual pas-sion for music. By age four he could pound out several bars of Wagner's *Ride of the Valkyries* on the piano.

For the next week Patrick practiced his stanza several times with his mother. A rehearsal at the church went well. Still, I could only envision myself at age five, singing into a microphone before hundreds of people. When Christmas Eve arrived, my expectations were limited.

Catherine, my daughter Melanie, and I sat with the congregation in darkness as a spotlight found my son, standing alone at the microphone. He was dressed in white, with a pair of angel wings.

Slowly, confidently, Patrick hit every note. As his voice washed over the people, he seemed a true angel, a true bestower of Christmas miracles.

There was eternity in Patrick's voice that night, a beauty rich enough to penetrate any nerve. At the sound of my son, heavy tears welled at the corners of my eyes.

His song was soon over, and the congregation applauded. Catherine brushed away tears. Melanie sobbed next to me.

After the service I moved to congratulate Patrick, but he had more urgent priorities. "Mom," he said as his costume was stripped away, "I have to go to the bathroom."

As Patrick disappeared, the pastor wished me a Merry Christmas, but emotion choked off my reply. Outside the sanctuary I received congratulations from fellow church members.

I found my son as he emerged from the bathroom. "Patrick, I need to talk to you about something," I said, smiling. I took him by the hand and led him into a room where we could be alone. I knelt to his height and admired his young face, the large blue eyes, the dusting of freckles on his nose and cheeks, the dimple on one side.

He looked at my moist eyes quizzically.

"Patrick, do you remember when you asked me why you had never seen me cry?"

He nodded.

"Well, I'm crying now."

"Why, Dad?"

"Your singing was so wonderful it made me cry." Patrick smiled proudly and flew into my arms.

"Sometimes," my son said into my shoulder, "life is so beautiful you have to cry."

Our moment together was over too soon. Untold treasures awaited our five-year-old beneath the tree at home, but I wasn't ready for the traditional plunge into Christmas just yet. I handed Catherine the keys and set off for the mile-long hike home.

The night was cold and crisp. I crossed a park and admired the full moon hanging low over a neighborhood brightly lit in the colors of the season. As I turned toward home, I met a car moving slowly down the street, a family taking in the area's Christmas lights. Someone inside rolled down a window.

"Merry Christmas," a child's voice yelled out to me.

"Merry Christmas," I yelled back. And the tears began to flow all over again.

We never understand the love of our parents until we become parents ourselves.

HENRY WARD BEECHER

A Place of Refuge

MELISSA MARIN
AGE 17

Have you ever had a day when things seem to be so over-whelming, you just have to get away? Those days come very often for me. I tend to get stressed easily. My favorite place of refuge was at my great-grandma's house. I could run there any time of the day and find open arms. She always knew how to make me laugh through my tears.

Grandma Laura had the prettiest garden in town. One day I said I wanted a garden of my own.

Grandma's face lit up. "Oh, Lissa," she said, "I have plenty of ideas." She grabbed my hand and took me back to the garage. She handed me all kinds of seeds: pansies, buttercups, marigolds, snapdragons, daisies, squash, and anything else you could imagine.

And then we walked through her early spring garden. For every plant she had a story to tell. She told me how it took two years before her daisies started. The rosebush was a peace offering from my grandfather when they had a disagreement. And her daughters and their friends picked her apples and then dipped them in caramel.

Then she led me to her prized bed of tulips. The beautiful reds and yellows and purples were always a place of serenity for me. We sat down and Grandma started another story.

"My parents couldn't afford to buy me a nice wedding present. So Mother dug up three tulip bulbs and gave them to me. I planted them in this very spot. And every time my daughters and granddaughters—and now my great-granddaughter—wanted to start a garden, I have dug up a tulip bulb, so that they can carry on the tradition."

She carefully placed a bulb into my hands. "Here, Lissa, start your own garden."

My garden flourished. I did, too, as I moved through my teen years, taking on leadership positions and playing several sports a year. But before I knew what was happening, I slowly started to drift away from her. Before I knew it, her eighty-seventh birthday arrived. I planned several times to visit but got sidetracked. Four nights later the call came. Grandma Laura had passed away. I was numb. I never said happy birthday. I never said good-bye. The place where I once laughed and cried no more existed.

The next few days were never ending. Sympathy cards, food trays, and company arrived every day. They only made the whole thing more real, and I didn't want to believe it. I couldn't step foot near her house. Life was gone from it—even the garden seemed still. The funeral finally came and went. Afterward I detached myself from others to survive. And that's about all I did—survive.

School in the spring is the most stressful time of year. Finals, makeup work, last-minute projects, not to mention all the problems girls go through with their friends—I was overwhelmed again. One May day seemed the worst. I had a physics exam, and after school I had to make up a Spanish test. Also, my best friend and I were in a fight. I drove around town. My eyes filled with tears. I needed to go somewhere. For some reason I drove to the cemetery.

I parked my car and got out. It was eerie being the only one there, but I kept walking. Then I saw it—my grandma's resting place. I sat down and began to pray. I told God everything—how much I missed her, how I hadn't been able to accept her death, how I still needed her and a place to go when I was overwhelmed.

Finally I prayed, "Could you please tell Grandma that I remembered her birthday, but I was too busy to stop and see her? Could you tell her I'm sorry?"

Somehow I felt a sense of relief and forgiveness. As I stood up, I started to hum my grandma's favorite song, "The Old Rugged Cross." As I sang, I knew she would live in my heart. And as I drove home, I realized that my refuge was now just a prayer away, and that God would always comfort me whenever I called out to Him.

It's in the dead of winter now a couple of years later. I'm even busier than before, and stress is a regular companion. Winter will soon turn into spring, and then I'm going to make another trip to the cemetery. There I'll rest a moment and smile at the beautiful blossoms—tulips that grew from bulbs I planted for Grandma Laura, who helped me remember that refuge is just a prayer away.

Weathered Love

NANCY SIMPSON

As a single mother, I have often wondered if my guidance has given my sixteen-year-old son what I consider to be a healthy basis for life.

The struggles to discipline, while offering a shoulder to cry on and an ear to listen, have been overwhelming. This balancing act of strength and tenderness has left me weary at times for the past thirteen years we've been on our own. However, the following event, which occurred several years ago, left me feeling very fulfilled in my role as both mother and protector.

It was the end of the school year and as is typical of living in the Midwest, the school had just held an all-day event on tornadoes and weather that often accompanies the spring months in Missouri. As luck would have it, soon after we had the experience of being awakened from our sleep by the sound of severe weather sirens ringing throughout our small little town.

Ryan knew exactly what we needed to take with us to the basement as we scurried for a safe haven. I grabbed the flashlight and small portable TV while he grabbed a blanket and his best buddy, Molly, our cat.

He was very calm and seemed to take his responsibilities in this potential disaster with great seriousness. As we made our way down the flight of stairs into the basement, he began to explain to me all the precautions and procedures that needed to be taken. During the class at school, the students had been instructed that the safest corner of the basement was the southwest corner.

As we approached the bottom of the stairs, Ryan conveyed this to me and then looking at me through the most protective eyes I've ever seen, he said, "You take that one, Mom." Not realizing that the southwest corner could be shared in this situation, his first thought was to protect his mother.

We made it through that night with a new respect for weather and the blessing of not actually experiencing a tornado, just a threat. But the act of love and selflessness my son gave me that night definitely blew me away.

Winter Nights

MARY SLAVKOVSKY
AGE 17

We never forget our past. Though it can be hazy, it is there. Childhood is the strong foundation on which we rely and build our futures.

I remember the long winter days when thick, massive icicles reached down from our poorly shingled roof to the bottom of our patio. It was Friday and I had just finished the half-mile walk from school to my house. My breath had moistened my scarf, and I was constantly sniffing. My hands were chilled. I had made the mistake of making snowballs wearing my mismatched knit gloves. My gloves were drenched and my hands were wetter and colder than the snow they had molded. My boots were too big, and snow had crept inside them and packed itself into ice cubes that rubbed against my bare ankles. The air was nippy and painfully cold as I trudged up the sidewalk to my porch. Stomping my boots, I released my feet from the excess snow they had been carrying. With a hard jolt to push the door open, I entered the living room.

Warmth immediately engulfed me and was welcomed by my wet, uncomfortable body. Over in the corner the furnace roared. Almost instinctively my frozen feet walked in front of it and I sat down. This furnace was the only heater in our entire house. During the winter we had no choice but to live in the living room. Our bunk beds were brought out from our rooms and set up against the walls. My parents put two army cots together to form their bed. A curtain was hung in the doorway of the living room to the kitchen to keep the scarce and much-needed heat in the living room.

To some this may seem like a miserable situation, living together cramped in one room with one heater in our cold house in the dead of winter, but for me it was different. I always remembered the winter as a time I grew close to my family. Because we all lived in the same room, we had to get along.

The remainder of my Friday was spent lost in a jungle of sheets, blankets, and beds. Squeals from my younger sister were heard as my older brother and I concentrated on the construction of a fort that would extend across the living room. The comforting smell of the crisp, freshly washed sheets was refreshing, and the laughter of my brother, sister, and me livened the cold, dreary house.

When it was time for bed, I snuggled down into the blankets and waited to be tucked in. My father brought his guitar out from behind his bed. We all lay in eagerness and waited to hear him sing. As his fingers softly strummed the six thin strings on his guitar and as his calming voice overtook the silence of the house, I began to relax. I felt my mother's soft touch as she stroked my back and hummed along. All the lights were off in the house, and when the playing stopped I received kisses from my parents. I whispered "I love you" to them both before cozily rolling over to face the wall to fall asleep. I drifted into a deep slumber while the furnace hummed at my feet.

This is a memory on which I have built my future. When times have been hard I always find myself remembering my childhood winter days. The winter taught me that life can be simple and enjoyable. It taught me what love is. The love my family showed during the winter days created a strong base for me to expand on and depend on. The happiness and safety gained from my family is there to guide my life story.

Dad Coming Home Was the Real Treat

HOWARD MANN

When I was a little boy I never left the house without kissing my parents good-bye. I liked kissing my mother because her cheek felt mushy and warm, and because she smelled of peppermints. I liked kissing my father because he felt rough and whiskery and smelled of cigars and witch hazel.

About the time I was ten years old, I came to the conclusion that I was now too big to kiss my father. A mother, okay. But with a father, a big boy should shake hands—man to man, you see.

He didn't seem to notice the difference or to mind it. Anyway, he never said anything about it. But then he never said much about anything except his business.

In retrospect, I guess it was also my way of getting even with him. Up until then I had always felt I was something special to him. Every day, he would come home from that mysterious world of his with a wondrous treat, just for me. It might be a miniature baseball bat, engraved with Babe Ruth's signature. It might be a real honeycomb with waffle-like squares soaked in honey. Or it might be exotic rahat, the delectable, jellied Turkish candies, buried in powdered sugar and crowded into a little wooden crate.

How I looked forward to his coming home each night! The door flung open and there he stood. I would run to him, hug him while he lifted me high in his arms.

I reached my peak the day of my seventh birthday. I woke up before anyone else in the family and tiptoed into the dining room. There, on the heavy mahogany table, was a small, square wristwatch with a brown leather strap, stretched out full length in a black velvet box. Could it really be for me? I picked it up and held it to my ear. It ticked! Not a toy watch from the five-and-dime, but a real watch like grown-ups wore. I ran into his bedroom, woke up father and covered him with kisses. Could any boy possibly be as happy as me?

Later, it began to change. At first, I wasn't aware it was happening. I suppose I was too busy with school and play and having to make new friends all the time. (We moved every two years, always seeking a lower rent.)

The flow of treats dried up. No more bats or honeycombs. My father gradually disappeared from my life. He would come home late, long after I had gone to sleep. And he would come home with his hands empty. I missed him very much, but I was afraid to say anything. I hoped that he would come back to me as strangely as he had left. Anyhow, big boys weren't supposed to long for their fathers.

Years after he died, my mother talked about how the Depression had "taken the life out of him." It had crushed his dream of being a "big man." He no longer had money for treats. He no longer had time for me.

I am sorry now. I look at his picture and his crinkly hazel eyes and wish that he were here today. I would tell him what is happening with me now and talk about things that he might like to hear—politics, foreign events and how business is doing. And I would put my arms around his neck and say, "Pop, you don't have to bring me anything—just come home early."

And I would kiss him.

Little Sister

MARTY WILKINS

I was seventeen years old before I understood the purpose of having a little sister. I mean, I loved my sister, and my mom says I adored her when I was real young. But for a boy growing up, a little sister is just not good for much. You can't play catch with her. If you want to play tag, she's too easy to catch so that's not much fun. I certainly did not want to play dollies, and she tattled on everything so I couldn't get away with squat. This doesn't mean I wasn't proud of her at times, or that we never talked; she just wasn't much use.

All that changed when I was seventeen and a senior in high school. Now, I was not particularly blessed with a rip-roaring social calendar my first three years in high school. I was very shy, loved sports, and was a good student, but I was petrified if someone came up and talked to me.

I remember the time when a girl I had a crush on was walking down the hall toward me. Mr. Cool, that's me, decided to take a detour into the boys' bathroom and avoid all potential contact. I misjudged the distance to the bathroom, however, and ended up turning square into an indentation in the hallway wall, missing the bathroom by a good six feet and planting my nose into a bulletin board. I then decided to just try and look cool like I was just trying to read a flyer on the bulletin board from real close. She walked by shaking her head and laughing. What a clod! Fortunately, God would send in reinforcements to the school to aid me in the quest for social acceptance. My little sister, Lori, became a freshman that year.

Now Lori had been making plans for my senior year which were unknown to me. The first Friday of the year meant our first home football game. I had planned to play in the game, eat pizza, and go home. Good solid strategy for remaining social inept for the rest of my high school career. Lori, however, had the gall to tell me that after the game, I was going to the dance. The number one most feared high school activity for one such as myself.

I said, "No, I'm not."

She said, "Yes, you are."

"No, I'm not."

"Yes, you are, because I'm going, you can drive, and I need a ride home."

After careful consideration of the fact that I would never win this battle, I found myself preparing for the after-game dance. (Mom and Dad would have backed up Lori completely. They were in that handful of high school parents who worried if their child was not out doing something on Friday and Saturday nights.)

The time for the dance arrived. I went in, stomach in knots, knees wobbly, and eagerly casing out all of the exits in case I cracked under the pressure. Well, Lori would have nothing to do with her brother being a wallflower so she pulled me out onto the floor and made me dance. And then, it happened, the purpose, the reason, the usefulness of my little sister. She...had friends. I might have been their test case that night, or maybe I was just a safe haven, but I had a blast. I began to develop a new confidence in myself and who I was. I even found a new role at school that I thoroughly enjoyed: big brother.

I have never looked at my sister the same way after my senior year of high school. I am eternally grateful that she did not, and would not, allow me to fall socially. She believed in me before I ever did. Growing up, I loved her as my sister, but I grew to cherish her as my friend. She taught me a great lesson in friendship that year. Don't ever let the people you love settle for second best. Encourage them, support them, use a big stick if you have to. But at all costs, show them how much they are worth.

Sharing the Pain

NANCY B. GIBBS

As we awoke that gloomy summer morning, I felt a strong sense of dread.

Going to the dentist was not one of my favorite activities, but the days when I was forced to take my twin sons for any type of medical or dental treatments mark some of the worst days of my life. As much as I dislike going myself, I'd trade places with them anytime.

The day turned out worse than I could have ever imagined. Between the two boys, they had eight wisdom teeth removed. Having two twenty-year-old boys moaning at the same time was not my idea of a day for celebrations. They were miserable as the dentist packed their mouths with white gauze.

After the procedure was complete and we received the dentist's instructions, we left his office and headed home. It took both my husband and myself to get them into the car and then inside the house when we arrived home.

Following the dentist's instructions, Chad and Brad sat up in the recliners, which were side by side in our living room. The moaning didn't cease as their groans filled every corner of the room. Strips of gauze were sticking out of both sides of their mouths.

Daisey, our five-pound toy poodle, had compassion for the boys when she heard them groaning. For a while, she stood and stared at them with her tail tucked. She was very quiet, as if she understood the pain that they were experiencing. When she turned to look at me, she possessed a look of sadness and little tears filled her eyes. For a long time we both stayed right beside them, just in case they had a need.

A little while later, Daisey disappeared. It was very unusual for her to leave my side. She's never very far from her master and best friend. I decided that she couldn't stand seeing the boys so sick, so she slipped off into another room to hide.

Just a few minutes later, to our surprise, Daisey returned to the living room.

She firmly held a white sock in her mouth. She stared at the boys while holding on to it with her teeth. Then she lay down on the floor facing them. She continuously cut her eyes from Chad to Brad and back to Chad. Daisey knew that there wasn't much she could do, but decided that she could share in their pain. After the bleeding stopped and the boys removed the gauze, Daisey retired her sock as well. It was soaking wet.

Many times when someone close to us is experiencing difficulties and hardships, we are not sure what we can do to help. Daisey taught me that we may not be able to correct every problem for everyone, but with God's help we can most definitely share in the pain.

When the boys felt better, Daisey jumped from one chair to the other, wagging her tail while gently licking their faces.

I'm not sure who was happier when a glimmer of hope returned to the room that day—Daisey or me.

Seeing Dad Through Different Eyes

MARGARET BECKER

After a long week of classes and two part-time jobs, I always loved sleeping in on Saturday mornings. But my father never slept in. It seemed he was always up doing some early-morning job around the house. This particular Saturday was no different.

Outside my bedroom window, Dad had decided to plant flowers. I tossed and rolled on my bed with each irritating clank of a shovel. Finally, unable to muffle the sounds, I looked out the window to see if he was about finished.

As I stared at him, my frustration soon melted away. For some reason—I'm not sure why—I saw Dad a bit differently this morning. He suddenly wasn't the guy who rose early on Saturday because he liked to, but because some family job had to be done. This morning I saw him as a dad who worked hard for his family—who worked hard for me.

As I watched him laboring away, memories began replaying in my mind, filling my eyes with tears. There he was, leaning over the dining-room table as he patiently checked the answers to my homework…I saw the lightness of his step at the yearly square dance…I felt his gentle hand on my fevered forehead….

As I watched the sweat dripping from his face, a dozen questions went through my head. How many Saturday mornings had I heard the dull thud of a shovel or the loud whir of the lawn mower? How many times had I rolled over for another half hour of sleep?

How many times had I told him I loved him? How many times had I assured him he was an excellent father, generous in important things like love and attention—and time? How many opportunities had I missed to show him I cared? With all these questions fresh in my mind, I slipped on my jeans and a shirt and headed for the back door.

I'll never forget the look on Dad's face when I came around the corner with the metal rake in hand.

"What are you doing up so early, Maggie?" he asked.

"I came out to help you, Dad." He smiled warmly—the kind of smile only a parent can give. And together we began to turn over new ground. With each pull of the rake, I felt a joy and excitement that only comes from paying back a long overdue debt of love.

I knew I was special to him—that he was pulling for me and praying for me during each of the small crises that came my way. It's what every little girl needs from a father.

DANAE DOBSON
FROM *WHAT MY PARENTS DID RIGHT*

Keep Looking Up

Far away there in the sunshine
are my highest aspirations.
I may not reach them,
but I can look up and see their beauty,
believe in them,
and try to follow where they lead.

LOUISA MAY ALCOTT

The Package Isn't Empty

LONNI COLLINS PRATT
FROM *HERE I AM, LORD*

Buzz was a brilliant football star in my hometown. Like fire falling from heaven. His movements almost magical. Buzz was destined to be the celebrity quarterback from a small town. In a small town, stars get lots of attention and usually end up blinded by their own sparkle. Not Buzz. He paid attention to the kids no one else ever noticed. He said nice things to other people—every single day, and he'd been doing it for as long as I had known him. He didn't have to try to be nice. It came naturally.

His smile was always ready. When you needed a hand to hold, or a shoulder to lean on, you could count on those wide shoulders and strong hands. Buzz was an all-around nice guy—and my best friend. The fuss that local and state newspapers made about his future never meant much to him. He loved football, but it wasn't his life. He would run his dad's hardware store someday, marry a local girl, be buried out of the same little parish where both of us had been baptized, confirmed, and schooled. It would be a good life, he'd say, and then smile a Buzz sort of smile that lifted one corner of his mouth and ended in a wink.

In our senior year, Buzz got a deal from a big school other boys would have died for. And he got all those little extras no one ever admitted boys like Buzz got from colleges. All wrapped up in promises, shining lights, marching bands. He was on his way up, headed for the big time. Buzz never changed, not really, not inside. But he started thinking about his future in terms of the promises and spotlight and sports cars. Words like "pro" and "Super Bowl" crept into our conversations. It was a bright dream—no one could blame him for riding it out of our small town as far as the dream would take him.

I was with his parents, along with a few other close friends from high school, the day Buzz started as quarterback in a televised game between long-standing rivals. This was the *big* game. It was Buzz's debut on national TV. The world was at his door.

Buzz was sacked hard on the first play. And he didn't get up. He didn't get up for a very long time. I held his mother's hand while his father paled. Then we saw him move. He sat up but didn't move his legs. One leg moved. The other didn't. Cameras zoomed in. Buzz glanced up. I saw one corner of his mouth lift in a painful smile, and a wink crinkled his all-American boy-next-door face. It was over, but we cheered anyway.

Buzz fractured his ankle. He never came back all the way. He finished college with honors and returned home. He was a tall, tired, Midwestern kid with a limp and a cowlick. The people who had built shrines to his athletic ability wouldn't return his phone calls.

The package, for all its trimming and ribbons and glitter, was empty. The dream came to a sudden, irreversible end. The marching band stormed off the field, and Buzz wasn't a star anymore.

Today he runs the hardware store with his ready smile, and he's still hugging people and grinning when the bottom falls out of his world, which it has a time or two.

He said later that he did get caught up in the hype for awhile, but sometime during his freshman year he realized, "…it just didn't amount to anything that really mattered. The promises were empty, the stories were lies spun for a small-town boy they thought didn't have a brain in his head."

He said he always knew that the people who loved him, the ones who mattered, were not the people pumping him with stories of fame and for-tune. They were his parents and family, his lifelong friends…the people at home.

He limped home where we still considered him a hero, not because of his football pizzazz, but because he wasn't a package glittering on the outside and empty inside. Buzz is a real human being who learned early and learned well how to live and love.

You can crush the ankle of a guy like that, and he'll walk. You can toss him off a football field, and he'll stay in the game of life with a grin. The package isn't empty, and he's the real thing.

True wealth is what you are, not what you have.

AUTHOR UNKNOWN

Courage on Ice

=◎=

SUSAN FAHNCKE

t was the end of the first period and my husband left to get snacks while I watched the break-time entertainment at the hockey arena. The entertainment usually consists of something goofy like sumo-wrestling, inner tube races across the ice, things like that.

As I watched the men glide out onto the ice, I wondered what game they were playing tonight. They poured out, each one seated on a sledlike apparatus, their legs strapped to the sled. They carried hockey sticks in each hand, cut to accommodate the shorter distance to the ice from their seat on the sleds. Then I heard the announcer's voice. He was saying something about the United States Paralympic Hockey team. I looked more closely and realized most of the players had missing legs, or only one leg, or were paralyzed from the waist down. The duo-hockey sticks were also duo-purpose. They used them to push themselves around the ice the way a skier uses poles.

My heart caught in my throat as it hit me what incredible courage these athletes had to possess to come in front of hockey fans. (Hockey fans are not notoriously sensitive people.) I held my breath while I waited to see the audience's reaction to the paralympic teams. As the players shuffled around the ice, their speed about half that of the team we had just been watching, I felt as if the world stood still and silent. The hockey players' faces were intense with concentration. I felt for them and knew how nervous they must be. The players often collided and tipped over. The game was much slower-paced than we were used to. The stadium was silent. I cringed while I waited for the rowdy, sometimes crude, hockey fans around me to make fun of or laugh at the unique way this type of hockey was being played. I felt oddly emotional at their vulnerability and fiercely protective of them. I wondered if I would hit the first person to boo them.

At first, no one made a sound. I had never heard the arena so still. And then as if ten thousand people suddenly shared the same thought, we rose to our feet as one. Thunder filled the arena as the cheers of encouragement and pounding applause reverberated throughout the stadium. I felt hot tears spring to my eyes. I was so in awe of the courage and incredible determination these athletes felt. Being the mother of a "special" child, I felt a deep and intense pride for these men. I could guess what great obstacles they must have overcome to be here tonight. How brave and how strong their spirits were to get out on the ice, in a place where people might ridicule them. I so admired their will and determination.

It was an inspiration. And a revelation. The people around me, who had only minutes ago been screaming insults at the opposing goalie, were now showing tremendous support and human compassion for such great athletes. Genuine love filled the arena. I was shocked and touched. Watching the short game between the two teams created out of the entire USA team was something to see. And the joy of the coach was clearly evident, supporting them from his wheelchair at the side of the rink. He was glowing with an intense pride.

When my husband returned, the short exhibition game was ending and the players were leaving the rink. The Zamboni was cleaning the ice and fans were yelling for the players to stay. My husband looked at me quizzically, and it was a couple of minutes before I could find my voice to tell him what I had just witnessed. It had been a magical few moments that I won't forget. It turned an ordinary, boisterous hockey game into a night of awe.

High Button Shoes

MARGARET JENSEN
FROM *THE GREATEST LESSON I'VE EVER LEARNED*

needed shoes! I *always* needed shoes! Papa traveled throughout the province of Saskatchewan to minister to the needs of the Scandinavian immigrants, so our bank account was Philippians 4:19: "My God shall supply all your needs." He did—but not always my way!

The arrival of the "missionary barrel" was an annual event in our home. Every outdated relic from the past seemed to find its way into that barrel: moth-eaten coats, hats with plumes and feathers, corsets with the stays, threadbare silks and satins, shoes of all sizes and shapes.

Mama used the hand-me-downs from the missionary barrel to make clothes for her children. She wasted nothing. Buttons, silks and furs were transformed into beautiful dresses and coats. The scraps were put together for pallets for the floor, or sewn into quilts. We never lacked quilts!

"Margaret," Papa called, "we have shoes!"

I started to run away. I had lived through enough missionary barrel debuts to know I probably wouldn't like the shoes Papa had found.

"I'm sure they won't fit." I kept running.

"Margaret!"

I stopped. I went to Papa and stared in horror when he held up the monstrosities—two pairs of high button shoes, a black pair and a brown

150

pair. Oxfords were "in"; button shoes were "out"!

"Try them on." Papa left no room for discussion.

I complained that they were too big.

"Ja, that is good. We'll put cotton in the toes. They'll last a long time." No one argued with Papa.

Mama sensed my distress and tenderly said, "Margaret, we prayed for shoes, and now we have shoes. Wear your shoes with a thankful and humble heart. It is not so important what you have on the feet, but it is very important where the feet go. This could be one of life's valuable lessons." (No ten-year-old is interested in "valuable lessons.")

I knew better than to argue with God and Mama on this point, but I had a plan. Papa's sermons on faith told of Moses and the crossing of the Red Sea, Daniel in the den of lions. "If you have faith, you can move mountains," Papa's voice echoed in my mind. I knew what to do.

I carefully placed the shoes (buttonhook included!) beside my bedroom door and prayed, "Oh God, keep Your mountains, but move my shoes. Thank You."

The next morning I fully expected the shoes to be gone. Was I in for a surprise. They were still there. Something went wrong! I had a strange suspicion that it might be related to Mama's "valuable lessons."

"Hurry, Margaret," Mama called. "Time for Sunday school."

I buckled up my galoshes over those awful high button shoes and reluctantly trekked off in the snow to Sunday school. *If I can keep my galoshes on, no one will see my horrible shoes,* I thought to myself. *Tomorrow I'll think of something else.*

Upon arriving at church, I carefully wiped off my galoshes and started into class. A booming voice called out, "Margaret, no one goes into Sunday school class with galoshes on. You're dripping."

Slowly I unbuckled my galoshes, and there I stood, for all the world to see, in my embarrassing old high button shoes. My face grew hot as I felt my classmates' silent pity.

Then my friend Dorothy came in, and she was also carefully wiping off her galoshes. The same voice of authority boomed out, "Dorothy, take off your galoshes. You're dripping."

Slowly, Dorothy removed her galoshes ... and stood before us in a pair of hand-knit socks. She had no shoes. There we were, two ten-year-old girls, learning life's "valuable lesson."

"Good morning, young ladies," came the crisp English accent of our beloved Sunday school teacher. Mr. Avery, a frail, elderly, blue-eyed gentleman with white hair and a goatee, quietly assessed the situation.

Each Sunday, as we formed a large circle in our class, Mr. Avery chose two children to sit beside him. It was almost like sitting next to God. This morning Mr. Avery announced, "Dorothy, you sit here on one side of me and Margaret, you sit here on the other."

The shoes and socks were forgotten. He had picked us! Mr. Avery had picked us! My old shoes and Dorothy's socks didn't matter to Mr. Avery. He had picked us anyway! I remember very little of what he said that morning—but I'll never forget what he did.

When it was time to leave, Dorothy and I pulled on our galoshes and walked out into the snow. Our heads were held high—Mr. Avery had picked us!

Mama was right. It is not so important what is on our feet, but where our feet go.

The Girl with the Apple

HERMAN AND ROMA ROSENBLAT
FROM *HEARTPRINTS*

it is bitter cold on this dark winter day in 1944. But it is no different than any other day in the Nazi concentration camp. Back and forth I pace, trying to keep my emaciated body warm. I am just a boy, and hungry. I have been hungry for longer than I want to remember. Edible food seems like a dream, and I sink deeper into despair.

Suddenly, I see something moving in the field; near the outer fence is a young girl. With an eye out for the guards, I hurry to the inside fence.

The girl stops working and looks at me with sad eyes—eyes that seem to say she understands. I ask, across twenty feet and two fences, if she has something to eat. She reaches into her pocket and pulls out a red apple. A beautiful, shiny red apple. She looks to the left and to the right and then with a smile of triumph, throws the apple over the fences. I pick it up, holding it with trembling, frozen fingers, then run away as fast as I can. If the guards see us, we will both be shot.

The next day, I cannot help myself—I am drawn at the same time to that spot near the fences. Am I crazy for hoping she will come again? Of course. But in here, I cling to any tiny scrap of hope.

She comes. And again, she brings an apple, flinging it over the fences with that same sweet smile. This time I catch it and hold it up for her to see. Her eyes twinkle. And for the first time in so long, I feel my heart move with emotion.

For seven months we meet like this. Sometimes we exchange a few words. Sometimes, just an apple. But she is feeding more than my belly, this angel from heaven. She is feeding my soul. And somehow, I know I am feeding hers as well.

One day I hear frightening news: We are being shipped to another camp. The next day when I greet her, my heart is breaking. I can barely speak. "Do not bring me an apple tomorrow," I say. "I am being sent to another camp. We will never see each other again." Turning before I lose all control, I run away. I cannot bear to look back. If I did, I know she would see tears streaming down my face.

Months pass, and the nightmare continues. Only the memory of this girl sustains me. And then one day, just like that, the nightmare is over. The war has ended. Those of us still alive are freed. I have lost everything precious to me, including my family. But I still have the memory of this girl, a memory I carry in my heart as I move to America to start a new life.

The years go by. It is 1957. I live in New York City. A friend convinces me to go on a blind date with a lady friend of his. Reluctantly, I agree. But she is nice, this woman named Roma. And like me, she is an immigrant, so we have at least that in common.

"Where were you during the war?" Roma asks me gently, in that delicate way immigrants ask one another such questions.

"I was in a concentration camp in Germany," I reply.

Roma gets a faraway look in her eyes.

"What is it?" I ask.

"I am just thinking about something from my past, Herman," Roma explains in a voice suddenly very soft. "You see, when I was a young girl, I lived near a concentration camp. There was a boy there, a prisoner, and for a long while, I used to visit him every day. I remember I used to bring him apples. I would throw the apple over the fence, and he would be so happy."

Roma sighs heavily and continues. "It is hard to describe how we felt about each other—after all, we were so young, and we only exchanged a few words when we could—but I can tell you, there was much love there. I assume he was killed like so many others. But I cannot bear to think that, and so I try to remember him as he was for those months we were given together."

With my heart pounding so hard I think it will explode, I look directly at Roma and ask, "And did that boy say to you one day, 'Do not bring me an apple tomorrow. I am being sent to another camp'?"

"Why, yes," Roma responds, her voice trembling. "But Herman, how on earth could you possibly know that?"

I take her hands in mine and answer, "Because I was that young boy, Roma."

For many moments, there is only silence. We cannot take our eyes from each other as we recognize the soul behind the eyes, the dear friend we once loved so much, whom we have never stopped loving.

Finally, I speak: "Roma, I was separated from you once, and I don't ever want to be separated from you again. Now I am free, and I want to be together with you forever. Dear, will you marry me?"

I see that same twinkle in her eye I used to see as Roma says, "Yes, I will marry you." We embrace—the embrace we longed to share for so many months, but barbed wire came between us. Now, nothing ever will again.

Sharing the Wonder

*If a man were to climb the highest peak
and survey all the wonders of the world,
their beauty would be diminished
if there were no one there to share it with.*

CICERO

True Height

DAVID NASTER

His palms were sweating. He needed a towel to dry his grip. A glass of ice water quenched his thirst, but hardly cooled his intensity. The Astroturf he was sitting on was as hot as the competition he faced today at the national Junior Olympics. The pole was set at seventeen feet. That was three inches higher than his personal best. Michael Stone confronted the most challenging day of his pole-vaulting career.

The stands were still filled with about 20,000 people, even though the final race had ended an hour earlier. The pole vault is truly the glamour event of any track-and-field competition. It combines the grace of a gymnast with the strength of a body builder. It also has the element of flying, and the thought of flying as high as a two-story building is a mere fantasy to anyone watching such an event. Today and now, it is not only Michael Stone's reality and dream—it's his quest.

As long as Michael could remember, he had always dreamed of flying. Michael's mother read him numerous stories about flying when he was growing up. Her stories were always ones that described the land from a bird's eye view. Her excitement and passion for details made Michael's dreams full of color and beauty. Michael had this one recurring dream. He would be running down a country road. He could feel the rocks and chunks of dirt at his feet. As he raced down the golden-lined wheat fields, he always outran the locomotives passing by. It was at the exact moment he took a deep breath that he lifted off the ground. He would soar like an eagle.

Where he flew always coincided with his mother's stories. Wherever he flew was with a keen eye for detail and the free spirit of his mother's love. His dad, on the other hand, was not a dreamer. Bert Stone was a hard core realist. He believed in hard work and sweat. His motto: If you want something, work for it!

From the age of fourteen, Michael did just that. He began a very careful and regimented weight-lifting program. He worked out every other day with weights, with some kind of running work on alternate days. The program was carefully monitored by Michael's coach, trainer, and father.

Michael's dedication, determination, and discipline were a coach's dream. Besides being an honor student and an only child, Michael Stone continued to help his parents with the farm chores. Michael's persistence in striving for perfection was not only his obsession, but his passion.

Mildred Stone, Michael's mother, wished he could relax a bit more and be that "free dreaming" little boy. On one occasion she attempted to talk to him and his father about this, but his dad quickly interrupted, smiled, and said, "You want something, work for it!"

All of Michael's vaults today seemed to be the reward for his hard work. If Michael Stone was surprised, thrilled, or arrogant about clearing the bar at seventeen feet, you couldn't tell. As soon as he landed on the inflated landing mat, and with the crowd on their feet, Michael immediately began preparing for his next attempt at flight. He seemed oblivious of the fact that he had just surpassed his personal best by three inches and that he was one of the final two competitors in the pole-vaulting event at the national Junior Olympics.

When Michael cleared the bar at seventeen feet, two inches and seventeen feet, four inches, again he showed no emotion. Constant preparation and determination were his vision. As he lay on his back and heard the crowd moan, he knew the other vaulter had missed his final jump. He knew it was time for his final jump.

Since the other vaulter had fewer misses, Michael needed to clear this vault to win. A miss would get him second place. Nothing to be ashamed of, but Michael would not allow himself the thought of not winning first place.

He rolled over and did his ritual of three finger-tipped push-ups along with three marine-style push-ups. He found his pole, stood, and stepped on the runway that led to the most challenging event of his seventeen-year-old life.

The runway felt different this time. It startled him for a brief moment. Then it all hit him like a wet bale of hay. The bar was set at nine inches higher than his personal best. That's only one inch off the national record, he thought.

The intensity of the moment filled his mind with anxiety. He began shaking the tension from his body. It wasn't working. He became tenser. Why was this happening to him now, he wondered. He began to get nervous. Fear would be a more accurate description. What was he going to do? He had never experienced these feelings.

Then out of nowhere, and from the deepest depths of his soul, he envisioned his mother. Why now? What was his mother doing in his thoughts at a time like this? It was simple. His mother always used to tell him that when you felt tense, anxious, or even scared, to take deep breaths.

So he did. Along with shaking the tension from his legs, he gently laid his pole at his feet. He began to stretch out his arms and upper body. The light breeze that was once there was now gone. He could feel a trickle of cold sweat running down his back.

He carefully picked up his pole. He felt his heart pounding. He was sure the crowd did, too. The silence was deafening. When he heard the singing of some distant robins in flight, he knew it was his time to fly.

As he began sprinting down the runway, something felt wonderfully different, yet familiar. The surface below him felt like the country road he used to dream about. The rocks and chunks of dirt, the visions of the golden wheat fields seemed to fill his thoughts.

When he took a deep breath, it happened. He began to fly. His take-off was effortless. Michael Stone was now flying, just like in his childhood dreams. Only this time he knew he wasn't dreaming. This was real. Everything seemed to be moving in slow motion. The air around him seemed the purest and freshest he had ever sensed. Michael was soaring with the majesty of an eagle.

It was either the eruption of the people in the stands or the thump of his landing that brought Michael back to earth. On his back with that wonderful hot sun on his face, he could only envision the smile on his mother's face. He knew his dad was probably smiling too, even laughing. Bert would always do that when he got excited: smile then sort of giggle. What he didn't know was that his dad was hugging his wife and crying.

That's right: Bert "if-you-want-it-work-for-it" Stone was crying like a baby in his wife's arms. He was crying harder than Mildred had ever seen before. She also knew he was crying the greatest tears of all: tears of pride.

Michael was immediately swarmed with people hugging and congratulating him on the greatest achievement thus far in his life. He later went on that day to clear seventeen feet and six and a half inches: National and International Junior Olympics records.

With all the media attention, endorsement possibilities, and swarming herds of heartfelt congratulations, Michael's life would never be the same. It wasn't just because he won the National Junior Olympics and set a new world record. And it wasn't because he had just increased his personal best by nine and a half inches. It was simply because Michael Stone is blind.

Class Spirit

JIM ZABLOSKI
FROM 25 MOST COMMON PROBLEMS IN BUSINESS

Mr. Alter's fifth-grade class at Lake Elementary School made headlines when the boys in the class decided to shave their heads. They did so, without embarrassment, because one of their own, Ian O'Gorman, developed cancer and had undergone chemotherapy. His hair began to fall out.

To make their friend feel at home, to feel one with the crowd, all his classmates agreed to shave their heads, with their parents' permission, so that upon his return, Ian would not stand out from the class. No one would know who the "cancer kid" was. The teacher, Mr. Alter, was so moved by the spirit of his class that he too shaved his head.

Grand Slam Hero

RETOLD BY ELIZABETH FARLEY

Do you think they will let me play?" Bennie asked his father.

The father and son were walking by the baseball diamond in the park. Some boys Bennie knew were into a rousing game of neighborhood ball. But Bennie knew his chances of playing in that game or any game were slim. He was a student from a school in Brooklyn, New York, that caters to learning disabled children.

Bennie's father was aware that his son was not an athlete and that he was a boy who was not likely to be chosen on any team. But he also knew that if his son could play for a team, it would be a boost to his fragile self-esteem and would give him a sense of belonging.

He approached a team member in the field.

"Do you suppose my son Bennie could play with you today?" he asked.

The boy looked around at his teammates for a consensus of opinion. No one responded.

He made a decision.

"We're losing this game by six runs, and we're in the eighth inning. I guess he could be on our team—we'll try to put him up to bat in the ninth."

Bennie grinned from ear to ear. He was told to put on a glove and to play short center field.

In the bottom of the eighth inning, Bennie's team scored a couple of runs, but was still behind by three. In the bottom of the ninth, his team scored again.

Now it was two out and the bases loaded! The potential winning run was on base.

Bennie was up next. Would the team actually let him have a turn and give up their chance to win the game?

Surprisingly, he was handed a bat. "Bennie, you're up!"

Bennie took the bat and stepped up to the plate. He didn't even know how to hold it properly, let alone hit the ball.

The pitcher moved up a few steps and softly lobbed the ball toward him, to at least give him a chance to make contact.

Bennie swung and missed by a mile.

One of his teammates walked up behind him quietly and positioned his hands over Bennie's on the bat. Together they held the bat, facing the pitcher.

The pitcher moved a few steps closer and again let the ball softly move toward the batter's box.

As the pitch came toward them, Bennie and his teammate swung.

Contact!

The slow ground ball made its way toward the pitcher and he picked it up. He could easily throw the ball to first in plenty of time, and the game would be over.

Instead, the pitcher threw a high arching ball to the right field, far over the first baseman's head.

"Run, Bennie, run!" Everyone was up and yelling. "Run to first!"

Never in his life had Bennie run to first base. He scurried down the baseline, startled and panting. By the time he reached the base, the right fielder had the ball. He could make an easy throw to second base for the tag out.

As Bennie was rounding first, the right fielder, understanding what the pitcher's intentions had been, threw the ball toward third, high over the third baseman's head.

"Run to second, Bennie. Get to second!" everyone screamed.

He sprinted toward second, while the base runners joyfully circled the bases and headed for home. As he approached second base, the opposing shortstop ran to him, turned toward third base and shouted, "Go on, Bennie, run to third!"

Bennie was gasping across the third base bag when the boys from both teams began running behind him, screaming, "Run for home, keep going for home!"

Bennie's feet crossed home plate, his body straining, his face bright red.

All eighteen players lifted him onto their shoulders, and carried him off the field, making him the hero who had just hit a "grand slam homer" to win the game for his team.

Bennie's father told this story as he stood before the crowd that had gathered at the annual fund-raising event for Bennie's school that year.

"Many times I have questioned God's purpose in the life of my son who cannot learn as other children can. Isn't God supposed to do everything with perfection? Where is God's perfection in this? But I believe that when God brings a child like this into the world, the perfection that he seeks is in the way people react to Bennie and others like him."

"And that day," he said softly, tears running down his cheeks, "those eighteen boys reached their level of God's perfection."

T. J.

GREGORY AND SUZANNE WOLFE
FROM *CLIMB HIGH, CLIMB FAR*

Once I was talking with my father about sacrifices, and whether anyone these days still thought they were important. He told me about a boy he grew up with, and the story impressed me so much that I tell it often, as an example of what human beings can be.

My father's friend was named T.J. Hulsey, and by all accounts he was not an extraordinary boy. He was from a very small Southern town, grew up in the country poverty typical in those regions that never quite recovered from the Depression, and had only the limited education such an environment could afford. He was of average build, average intelligence, quiet disposition, and enjoyed the same activities all the boys of his time and place experienced: hunting, fishing, and simply standing around the town square on hot afternoons. He was not a leader in school or in his group of friends. He was someone everyone knew, but he was not the first person who came to mind.

When the Korean War broke out, T.J., who was around eighteen, was drafted into the service. He spent his time in the army, going through basic training for six weeks, and performing in his usual satisfactory, though not stellar manner. When time came for assignments, T.J. was called as one of the men to be sent overseas, to one of the hottest areas of fighting, along the Chinese-Korean border.

Reports of battle could not be overestimated. The Chinese had entered the fray to support the North Korean army; American troops found themselves in the midst of an overwhelming assault from the north. Casualties were a given, deaths an inevitability.

Like all outfits sent into such a situation, T.J.'s group was to hold off the advances as best they could. Unfortunately, the enemy forces were superior in number and position.

A day came when the fighting was particularly fierce. T.J.'s outfit was in steady retreat. The enemy forces were closing in from the front and threatened to overrun the Americans. Though they fell back from their positions as fast as they could, the Chinese-Korean advance was too fast. T.J.'s platoon was to be overrun in a matter of minutes; their deaths were a certainty. The only way to salvage the situation was for the men to stop trying to defend themselves and make an all-out effort at retreat. Without any fire cover, however, their survival would be nearly impossible.

It was then that this unremarkable boy, who'd never done anything of special note, who'd fought, like all the others, after the fashion of a machine, did something very unlike a machine—something rare, something human.

"Just leave me with your guns," he said, "and all the ammunition you got—I'll hold 'em off while y'all run."

In the little time that was left, there were arguments with T.J.—futile debates to make him change his mind. But in the end, the men knew that unless one of them sacrificed himself, none could live. They agreed, leaving T.J. with their weapons. Under T.J.'s fire cover, the boys made their escape. The noise was tremendous, one of them later reported, and the last time anyone saw T.J., he was standing on a bunker, using an empty rifle as a club to fend off the swarming enemy.

As has happened countless other times in countless other places, when T.J.'s body was returned to the town, people came to meet it. And as for any other boy, there was a dignified service, a flag on the coffin, and heartfelt condolences for the family. But, in addition, there were also a large number of military leaders at the funeral, who'd heard of T.J.'s act, and a squadron of pilots who flew over the graveyard in homage. A cascade of letters was delivered, from the families of the boys whose lives T.J. had ransomed. In time, there was also the highest honor a man can receive for military service—a medal commemorating the sacrifice of a life for a country and its people. All this for a quiet fellow of average abilities; someone who, by all accounts, was really an unremarkable boy.

When we forget ourselves,
we usually do something everyone else remembers.

AUTHOR UNKNOWN

The Art Collection

AUTHOR UNKNOWN

Y ears ago, there was a very wealthy man who, with his devoted young son, shared a passion for art collecting. Together they traveled around the world, adding only the finest art treasures to their collection. Priceless works by Picasso, Van Gogh, Monet, and many others adorned the walls of the family estate. The widowed elderly man looked on with satisfaction as his only child became an experienced art collector. The son's trained eye and sharp business mind caused his father to beam with pride as they dealt with art collectors around the world.

As winter approached, war engulfed the nation and the young man left to serve his country. After only a few short weeks, his father received a telegram. His beloved son was missing in action. The art collector anxiously awaited more news, fearing he would never see his son again. Within days, his fears were confirmed. The young man had died while rushing a fellow soldier to a medic.

Distraught and lonely, the old man faced the upcoming Christmas holidays with anguish and sadness. The joy of the season that he and his son had looked forward to would no longer visit his house. On Christmas morning, a knock on the door awakened the depressed, old man. As he walked to the door, the masterpieces of art on the walls only reminded him that his son was not coming home. As he opened the door, he was greeted by a soldier with a large package in his hands. He introduced himself to the man saying, "I was a friend of your son. I was the one he was rescuing when he died. May I come in for a few moments? I have something to show you."

As the two began to talk, the soldier told of how the man's son had told everyone of his, not to mention his father's, love of fine art. "I am an artist," said the soldier, "and I want to give you this." As the old man unwrapped the package, the paper gave way to reveal a portrait of the man's son. Though the world would never consider it the work of a genius, the painting featured the young man's face in striking detail. Overcome with emotion, the man thanked the soldier and promised to hang the picture above the fireplace.

A few hours later, after the soldier had departed, the old man set about his task. True to his word, he placed the painting above the fireplace, pushing aside thousands of dollars worth of art. His task complete, the old man sat in his chair and spent Christmas gazing at the gift he had been given.

During the weeks and months that followed, the man realized that even though his son was no longer with him, the boy's life would live on because of those he had touched. He would soon learn that his son had rescued dozens of wounded soldiers before a bullet stilled his caring heart. As the stories of his son's gallantry continued to reach him, fatherly pride and satisfaction began to ease his grief. The painting of his son soon became his most prized possession, far eclipsing any interest in the pieces for which museums around the world clamored. He told his neighbors it was the greatest gift he had ever received!

The following spring, the old man became ill and passed away. The art world was in anticipation, that with the collector's passing, and his only son dead, those paintings would be sold at auction. According to the will of the old man, all of the artworks would be auctioned on Christmas Day, the day he had received the greatest gift.

The day soon arrived and art collectors from around the world gathered to bid on some of the world's most spectacular paintings. Dreams would be fulfilled this day; greatness would be achieved as many would claim, "I have the greatest collection."

The auction began with a painting that was not on any museum's list. It was the painting of the man's son.

The auctioneer asked for an opening bid, but the room was silent.

"Who will open the bidding with $100?" he asked. Minutes passed, and no one spoke. From the back of the room came a voice, "Who cares about that painting? It's just a picture of his son."

"Let's forget about it and move on to the good stuff," more voices echoed in agreement.

"No, we have to sell this one first," replied the auctioneer. "Now, who will take the son?"

Finally, a neighbor of the old man spoke. "Will you take ten dollars for the painting? That's all I have. I knew the boy, so I'd like to have it."

"I have ten dollars. Will anyone go higher?" called the auctioneer. After more silence, the auctioneer said, "Going once, going twice, gone." The gavel fell.

Cheers filled the room and someone exclaimed, "Now we can get on with it, and we can bid on the real treasures!"

The auctioneer looked at the audience and announced that the auction was over. Stunned disbelief quieted the room. Someone spoke up and asked, "What do you mean, it's over? We didn't come here for a picture of some old guy's son. What about all of those other paintings? There are millions of dollars' worth of art here! We demand that you explain what is going on!"

The auctioneer replied, "It's very simple. According to the will of the father, whoever takes the son...gets it all!"

Puts things into perspective, doesn't it? Just as those art collectors discovered on Christmas Day, the message is still the same. Christmas is about the love of God, the Father, whose greatest joy came from his Son who went away and gave his life rescuing others. Because of that Father's love...whoever takes the Son gets it all!

I THINK OUR INSTRUCTOR IS A CHRISTIAN.
HE PRAYED THE WHOLE TIME I WAS DRIVING.

FOR MY EXTRA-CURRICULAR ACTIVITY
I'M GOING OUT FOR EXTREME CHESS.

THIS ONE SMELLS LIKE OLD PIGSKIN LEATHER.
I'VE BEEN TRYING TO GET A DATE WITH THE
CAPTAIN OF THE FOOTBALL TEAM.

HOMEWORK CAN BE "A PAIN IN THE BACK!"

SHE DRANK DECAF, I DRINK REGULAR.
WE JUST COULD NEVER FIND A
COMMON GROUND.

MEAT, DAIRY, VEGETABLES, BREAD...
I JUST REALIZED THAT PIZZA
HAS ALL FOUR FOOD GROUPS!

DE-FRAGMENT THE HARD-DRIVE, BACK UP THE FILES...
MY COMPUTERS MOTHERBOARD CAN BE SUCH A NAG.

YOU KIDS HAVE IT SO EASY WITH COMPUTERS
AND THE INTERNET. IN MY DAY WE DID REPORTS
THE OLD FASHIONED WAY. *WE* COPIED THEM BY HAND OUT
OF THE ENCYCLOPEDIA.

Yeah, You Make a Difference

One voice can make a song.
One life can change the world.

AUTHOR UNKNOWN

Eighteen Years Late

MICHAEL T. POWERS

What I remember most about junior high is the incredible pain and heartache that students inflicted on one another with their words and actions. There were students who seemed to have it all together and made those around them feel as if they didn't measure up. It wasn't until much later that I learned that those who ripped on others suffered from a terrible self-image, so in order to make themselves feel better, they tore others down. In fact, they were usually a totally different person from the one they presented to the outside world.

I didn't have the best self-image in junior high, and there were two things that I fell back on to be accepted: athletics and humor. I have always been a decent athlete, which brought a certain confidence and comfort level in my life, and I have always been able to make people laugh. At times the laughter came at another's expense, unfortunately, and most times I didn't fully realize what I was doing to the self-images of those around me, particularly one classmate of mine.

Her name was Tracy and she had a crush on me. Instead of nicely letting her know that I wasn't interested in her, I got caught up in trying to be funny, with her being the brunt of my jokes. I am ashamed now to think of how I treated her. I went out of my way to make things miserable for her. I made up songs about her and even wrote short stories in which I had to save the world from Tracy the evil villain.

That all changed about halfway through the year, however. Mr. Greer, my physical education teacher, came up to me one day.

"Hey, Mike, you got a second?"

"Sure, Mr. Greer!" I said. Everybody loved Mr. Greer, and I looked up to him like a father.

"Mike, I heard a rumor that you were going around picking on Tracy?" He paused and looked me straight in the eye. It seemed like an eternity before he continued.

"You know what I told the person I heard that from? I told them it couldn't possibly be true. The Mike Powers I know would never treat another person like that. Especially a young lady."

I gulped, but said nothing.

He gently put his hand on my shoulder and said, "I just thought you should know that." Then he turned and walked away without a backward glance, leaving me to my thoughts.

That very day I stopped picking on Tracy.

I knew that the rumor was true, and that I had let my role model down by my actions. More importantly, though, it made me realize how badly I must have hurt this girl and others for whom I had made life difficult.

It was probably a couple of months later before I fully realized the incredible way in which Mr. Greer had handled the problem. He not only made me realize the seriousness of my actions, but he did it in a way that helped me to save some of my pride. My respect and love for him grew even stronger after that.

I don't think I ever apologized to Tracy for my hurtful words and actions. She moved away the next year, and I never saw her again. While I was very immature as a seventh grader, I still should have known better. In fact, I did know better, but it took the wisdom of my favorite teacher to bring it out into the light.

So, Tracy, if you're out there, I am truly sorry for the way that I treated you, and I ask for your forgiveness—something I should have done eighteen years ago.

Ivy's Cookies

CANDY ABBOTT

The clank of the metal door and the echo of their footsteps rang in the ears of Ivy and Joanne as they walked down the dingy corridor behind the prison guard toward the "big room." The aroma of Ivy's homemade chocolate chip cookies wasn't enough to override the stench of ammonia from the recently mopped floor or the bitterness and anger that hung in the air. Women's Correctional Institute was not the kind of place where seventeen-year-olds go for an outing, but Ivy had a mission.

She didn't know what she was getting into, but she had to try. With trembling fingers, she dialed the number for an appointment at the prison. Warden Baylor was receptive to Ivy's desire to visit and referred her to Joanne, another teen who had expressed interest.

"How do we do this?" Ivy asked.

"Who knows? Maybe homemade cookies would break the ice," Joanne suggested.

So they baked their cookies and here they were, bearing gifts to strangers.

"I put almonds in these," Ivy rambled nervously as they moved along. "The dough was gummier than usual…"

"Don't chatter," the guard snapped. "It gets the prisoners riled."

The harsh words made Ivy jump and her heart pound. She walked the rest of the distance in silence.

"Okay. Here we are," the guard grunted, keys rattling. "You go in. I'll lock the door behind you. Be careful what you say. They have a way of using your words against you. You have fifteen minutes. Holler if you have any trouble."

Ivy noted the prisoners' orange jumpsuits and felt overdressed. Maybe we shouldn't have worn heels, she thought. They probably think we're snobs.

Remembering the guard's admonition, the girls put the cookies on the table next to plastic cups of juice without a word. Some prisoners leaned against the wall; others stood around—watching. Studying. Thinking. Staring. Nobody talked. Ivy smiled at one of the women, and she scowled back. From then on, she avoided eye contact. After five minutes of strained silence, Joanne whispered, "Let's move away from the table. Maybe they'll come over."

As they stepped back, one of the prisoners blurted out, "I'm gettin' a cookie." The others followed and began helping themselves. Soon they heard the rattle of keys. Time was up.

"What a relief to get outta there," Joanne sighed as a gust of fresh air caressed their perspiring faces.

"Yeah," Ivy agreed. "But there's a tug inside me that says we're not done. Would you be willing to go back?"

Joanne nodded with a half-smile. "How about Thursday after school?"

Week after week they came. And week after week the prisoners ate the cookies, drank the juice, and stood around in silence. Gradually, antagonistic looks were replaced by an occasional smile. Still, Ivy couldn't bring herself to speak—not a word.

Then one Thursday, an evangelist walked in. Her step was sure, her chin was high, and she glowed with the love of God. But she meant business. "I've come to pray with you," she announced. "Let's make a circle."

Ivy was awed by the inmates' compliance. Only a few resisted. Others, although murmuring, inched their way toward the middle of the room and formed a lopsided circle, looking suspiciously at one another.

"Join hands," the evangelist instructed. "It's not gonna hurt ya, and it'll mean more if you do." Slowly they clasped hands, some grasping hard, others barely touching. "Now, bow your heads." Except for the orange outfits, it could have been a church meeting.

"Okay. We're gonna pray," she continued, "and prayer is just like talking, only to God. I want to hear you tell the Lord one thing you're thankful for. Just speak it out. Don't hold back."

Ivy's palms were sweaty. *I can't pray out loud, Lord. I can't even talk to these women. Guess I should set an example, but they probably don't even like me—think I'm better than them 'cause of my clothes.*

The words of an inmate jolted her from her thoughts.

"I'm thankful, God, for Miss Ivy bringing us cookies every week."

Another voice compounded the shock, "God, thanks for bringing a black lady to see us, not just Quakers and Presbyterians."

Ivy's eyes brimmed with tears as she heard, "Thank you, God, for these two ladies givin' their time every week even though we can't do nothin' to pay 'em back."

One by one, every inmate in the circle thanked God for Ivy and Joanne. Then Joanne managed to utter a prayer of gratitude for the prisoners' words. But when it came Ivy's turn, she was too choked up to speak. Her eyes burned in humble remorse over how wrong she'd been about these women. She wished she could blow her nose, but the inmates were squeezing her hands so tightly, she resorted to loud sniffles and an occasional drip.

The following week, Ivy and Joanne returned, bright-eyed, to find the prisoners talkative.

"Why do you bring us cookies every week?" a husky voice inquired from the corner of the room. When Ivy explained, she inched a few steps closer. "Can you get me a Bible?" she asked. Others wanted to know more about the Jesus who inspires teenagers to visit prisoners.

A ministry was born from Ivy's cookies. What started as a silent act of kindness and obedience turned into a weekly Bible study at the prison which eventually grew so big it split into several groups that continue to this day. After Joanne married and moved away, Ivy continued to minister to the inmates alone for years. Eventually Prison Fellowship picked up the baton.

Ivy is a grandmom now. Her radiance has increased over the years, and she brightens any room she enters. But last Thursday afternoon she indulged herself in a good cry. Curled up on the couch, wrapped in the afghan her daughter had made, she wept. Deep sobs racked her body as she remembered it had been one year since her daughter died of asthma. She ached over the loss and felt, for the first time, the full weight of her words, "The kids can live with me." The baby was asleep in his crib and the two girls were in school when the doorbell rang.

There stood a young woman, probably seventeen, with a plate of homemade cookies.

"Are you Ivy Jones?" she asked.

"Yes," she answered, dabbing her eyes with a wadded tissue.

"These are for you," the girl said as she handed the cookies to her with a shy, sad smile, turning to leave without another word.

"Thank you," Ivy whispered in a daze. The girl was halfway down the sidewalk when Ivy called out, "But why?"

"My grandmother gave me her Bible before she died last week, and her last words were, 'Find Ivy Jones and take her some homemade cookies.'"

As the girl walked away, a wave of precious memories, uncertainties, and younger days flooded Ivy's soul. Swallowing the lump in her throat, she choked back a sob and headed toward the phone. *It's been a long time since I talked with Joanne.*

A Brother's Love

ALISON PETERS

The little Down syndrome girl, a teenager the size of a ten-year-old, made her way through the McDonald's restaurant to the back and turned toward the restroom. After stopping and looking closely at the word on the door to make absolutely certain she was entering the appropriate one, she walked in.

This was a happy evening for her. She and her family had just come from the roller rink with a group of friends from her church, and although trying to stay in an upright position while skating had been more work than fun for her, she knew now that it was certainly well worth the effort. After all, was there any place in the world offering greater rewards than McDonald's?

Her younger, but bigger, brother sat quietly. He noticed something that, thankfully, she had not noticed.

A group of four teenagers, two couples, had taken an interest in the little girl from the moment they spotted her. Their eyes were on her like magnets as she walked to the bathroom, and they snickered and whispered behind their hands, with one openly laughing, another pointing. Her brother watched them for a minute or so.

Then, he stood slowly, almost wearily, and walked casually across the restaurant to the booth where the four teens were sitting. The two guys paled slightly, and the girls looked a little alarmed as this total stranger placed his hands boldly on their table, leaning down slightly toward them. They studied each other while he was clearly in their space, and while they were most definitely out of their comfort zones. The stoic intruder stood up straight after several seconds and motioned with one hand for one of the couples to move over. He intended to sit right down next to them. Somewhat in shock, and thrown completely off guard, they made space for him as he lowered himself and sat down, hunched slightly forward with his forearms resting on the table.

"I was watching you making fun of my sister," he quietly informed them.

All four faces were now pale and the boys stumbled over their words in their rush to defend themselves.

"Who? Your sister? Where?"

"We weren't making fun of anyone!"

"Oh, that was your sister? We weren't making fun of her!"

"We would never make fun of someone like that!"

But he told them again, "I watched you."

They babbled whatever came to their minds, knowing they had been caught red-handed and maybe, just maybe, even realizing that they had been not only rude, but cruel to boot. Maybe they even got a little glimpse of the love this fifth wheel had for his sister, and an inkling of the emotions he was dealing with. Maybe.

The brother appeared not to be listening to their denials as he turned and watched his sister head back to where she had been sitting with the church group. Each of the four looked away, making sure they looked absolutely anywhere other than that little girl.

Somehow, on her return trip from the restroom, not one of them found her the least bit amusing. Her brother watched her sit down with the others, then he slid out of the booth and stood. As he turned to walk away, one of the boys tried for one last line of defense. "Hey, we would not make fun of her. We feel sorry for people like that!"

The little girl's defender stopped and turned back to their table and placing the palms of his hands again on its surface, he leaned in close to his new acquaintances, and said hoarsely, "And I feel sorry for people like *you.*"

Then he turned and walked away. And somehow, he suddenly blended in with the Happy Meal atmosphere as he took his place next to his little sister—just as if he were your average, basic McDonald's customer, and not a hero at all.

*Nobody made a greater mistake
than he who did nothing
because he could only do a little.*

EDMUND BURKE

Mrs. Warren's Class

COLLEEN TOWNSEND EVANS
FROM *START LOVING THE MIRACLE OF FORGIVING*

One of the great joys in life comes from watching a troubled person turn and go in a new and better direction. What causes such a thing to happen? A miracle? Sometimes. Forgiveness? Always!

Tom was a charming child, as most rascals are—but he was rebellious, a prankster, a rule breaker, a flaunter of authority. By the time he entered high school, his reputation had preceded him and he filled most of the teachers with dread. He took a special delight in disrupting classes and driving teachers to the limits of their patience. At home, he also was a problem. There were frequent confrontations between parents and child, each one seeking to prove he was more powerful than the other.

So many complaints were filed against Tom that the high school principal decided he would have to expel him—unless a teacher named Mrs. Warren agreed to take him into her class. Mrs. Warren was an exceptionally capable English teacher, but she also was a loving, endlessly patient woman who seemed to have a way with problem students. Yes, Mrs. Warren said, she would find a place for him in her eleven o'clock English literature class and also in her homeroom. She listened calmly as the principal read from a list of Tom's misdemeanors—a long list that had the principal shaking his head as he read. No, Mrs. Warren said, she wouldn't change her mind. She knew what she was getting into—she had heard about the boy.

When Tom was transferred to Mrs. Warren's class, he behaved as he always did upon meeting a new teacher. He slouched in his seat in the last row and glared at her, daring her by his attitude to do something about him. At first Mrs. Warren ignored him. Then, as the class began to discuss the reading assignment, Tom whispered a joke to the boy in front of him, making the boy laugh. Mrs. Warren looked up. Then she closed her book, stood, and placed another chair at the desk, next to hers.

"Tom, come up here and sit with me for a while," she said—not as a reprimand, but as a friend. It was an invitation she was offering, and her manner was so sweet that Tom couldn't refuse. He sat next to her as she went on with the lesson. "Tom is new to our class and hasn't had time to read the assignment, so if you'll bear with me, I'll read it out loud to him."

With Tom next to her, sharing her book, Mrs. Warren began to read from *A Tale of Two Cities*. She was a fine reader and captured Dickens' sense of drama magnificently. Tom, for all his determination to be an obstruction, found himself following the text, losing himself in the unfolding of a great story, sharing the excitement of it with a woman who really seemed to care about his interest in the book. That evening he startled his parents by sitting down without any prodding to do his homework—at least the assignment for Mrs. Warren's class.

That was only the beginning...Tom never missed a day of school after that first day in Mrs. Warren's class. Sometimes he cut other classes but never hers. He sat in the front row, participated in discussions, and seemed to enjoy reading aloud when he was called upon to do so. His appetite for reading suddenly became ravenous, and he asked Mrs. Warren to make up a list of books she thought he'd enjoy in his free time. After school he stayed in the classroom when the other students went home and had long talks with Mrs. Warren about the things he had read and the ideas they stimulated.

Tom wasn't exactly an angel in other classes, but the effect of his behavior in Mrs. Warren's class began to rub off a little—for which the other teachers were most grateful.

Tom didn't finish high school. In his junior year, after an angry outburst at home, he defiantly joined the Navy. He didn't even say good-bye to Mrs. Warren, who was very sad to see him leave school, because she thought she had failed in her attempt to reach him.

Seven years later, when Mrs. Warren was closing up her desk one afternoon before leaving for home, a young man came to the doorway and stood there, smiling. He was much taller and more muscular now, but Mrs. Warren recognized him within seconds. It was Tom! He rushed to her and hugged her so hard her glasses slid down her nose.

"Where have you been?" she said, adjusting her glasses and looking at him intently.

My—he was so clear-eyed, so happy and self-confident! "In school," he said, laughing.

"Sure, you thought I was in the Navy.... Well, I was, for a while. I went to school there."

It was a long story he had to tell. Thanks to the Navy he was able to finish high school...and then he went on to college courses. When his enlistment was up he got a job and continued his education at night. During that time he met a lovely girl. By the time he graduated he was married and had a son. Then he went on to graduate school, also at night.

"Well, what are you doing with your fine education?" Mrs. Warren asked.

"I'm a teacher—I teach English...especially to kids who disrupt other classes."

Tom had never forgotten the feeling of acceptance he had had from that first day in Mrs. Warren's class. More than all the threats, all the arguments and confrontations he had known, her forgiving love got through to him. And now he was passing that love on to other young people. He had learned the give-and-take of forgiveness.

Life's Pathway

What sunshine is to flowers,
smiles are to humanity.
They are but trifles to be sure,
but scattered along life's pathway,
the good they do is inconceivable.

JOSEPH ADDISON
FROM *IN THE COMPANY OF FRIENDS*

One Person

LONNI COLLINS PRATT
FROM *HERE I AM, LORD*

The elderly member of the hospital's housekeeping staff was known for showing visitors the basement of the institution. In that dingy reminder of the past she showed visitors what looked like small prison cells with rusty bars.

She pointed and said, "That's where they used to keep Annie."

Annie was brought here when she was a young woman because her family thought she was incorrigible, which means they couldn't control her. She'd bite and scream; she threw her food at people. The doctors and nurses couldn't even examine her without her scratching and hitting and throwing herself around.

I was only a few years younger than Annie, and I used to think how much I'd hate being locked up like that. I wanted to help, her screams were so horrible, but what could I do? I didn't know what to do, so I just did something I'm good at and baked her some brownies. I put them near her cell telling her they were for her and if she wanted them she could have them.

After that I'd talk to her sometimes, once I even got her laughing. She started behaving a little nicer when I was around. One of the nurses noticed it and asked if I would help them with Annie. Whenever they wanted to examine her I would go in the cage, calm her down, and hold her hand. That's how they discovered she was almost blind. She was glad for the discovery and felt that her actions had made a little bit of difference.

That's not the end of the maid's story though. The hospital tried to work with Annie, but it was still pretty tough. Then the Perkins Institute for the Blind opened. Annie was taught how to take care of herself; she was encouraged to learn independence and she grew into a confident, strong woman. She studied hard and became a teacher. Years later Annie returned to where she had been locked up and offered her assistance as a teacher.

They had just received a letter from a man who wanted help with his daughter. She was unruly, both blind and deaf, and she was more than he could deal with. He wondered if they knew anyone who could live with them and teach his daughter.

So Annie Sullivan became the teacher and lifelong companion of Helen Keller.

When Helen received the Nobel Prize she was asked who had the greatest impact on her life. Predictably, she answered it was Annie Sullivan. Annie corrected her, "No, Helen, the person who has had the most difference and impacted both our lives was a maid at the Tewksbury Institute."

The Lesson

TERESA OLIVE

Occasionally, a teacher comes along who can lift students out of the dreary routine of their workbook exercises and tests—a teacher who views education as an exciting journey and a lifelong process of discovery.

In my sophomore year of high school, I was blessed with such a teacher. Her name was Mrs. Roberts, though some of the seniors still slipped and called her by her maiden name.

Her recent marriage had surprised most of us, since we "mature" high schoolers considered anyone over forty too ancient for such things as romance. However, her newly acquired habit of humming in the halls indicated that she had adjusted quite well to married life. In fact, some of the seniors grumbled that we sophomores had it easy compared to what her classes had been like before she hummed in the halls.

It isn't that she was mean; it's just that she seemed to expect the impossible. Somehow, most of us managed to have accomplished nine years of school without learning how to write a decent paragraph, and Mrs. Roberts intended to change that state of affairs.

We dissected *Newsweek* and *Time* articles as if they were frogs in biology class. But our daily assignments were still returned with more red ink than black—most of it used to cross out words, phrases, even entire paragraphs. "Unnecessary" and "overly descriptive" words were Mrs. Roberts' enemies, and she attacked them ruthlessly.

In spite of our complaints, though, we really liked Mrs. Roberts. She didn't teach English as a way to make a living. She taught it because she was committed to it—and to us. She was determined to push us out of our cozy nest of complacent ignorance, knowing we were meant to fly.

Then one day she was absent. The whispered news spread across the room: Mrs. Roberts' husband had been killed in a car accident by a drunk driver who had veered into his lane, hitting him head-on.

Five days later, when Mrs. Roberts came back, she didn't hum as she came down the hall, but otherwise she acted as if nothing unusual had happened.

"Turn to page 97," she ordered in her usual brisk voice. The sound of rustling pages seemed amplified by the awkward silence. Finally, two girls in the front row stepped up to her desk and one of them stammered, "Mrs. Roberts, we—we're really sorry about what happened."

Her face contorted, Mrs. Roberts failed in her struggle for control and dropped her head on her desk, her shoulders heaving. The two girls gently patted her back as the rest of us watched helplessly.

When she at last regained some composure, she wiped off her glasses, looked at us and said, "I'm sorry. I thought I could handle this on my own, but I see now that I can't. You'll just have to bear with me for a while."

The tension was dissolved in a chorus of reassuring voices. "That's okay, Mrs. Roberts. Don't worry about us."

"All right," she said, putting back her glasses along with her best no-nonsense voice. "Let's get back to dangling participles."

That was the day that woke most of us to the strange notion that grown-ups could be vulnerable, too. Students often gathered around Mrs. Roberts between classes. Sometimes she would show them her husband's picture, which she kept in a locket around her neck. Tears became less frequent, but when they did slip out, someone would murmur an encouraging word.

Mrs. Roberts was a rare teacher. She taught us to be better writers. Even now, when I write, I can hear her crisp voice: "If it isn't necessary, cross it out." More important, though, she taught us that our need for each other is not our weakness, but rather our strength. After all, when something is crossed out, that which remains means more than ever.

*Give the world the best you have,
and the best will come back to you.*

MADELINE BRIDGES

Changing the World

When I was a young man, I wanted to change the world.

I found it was difficult to change the world, so I tried to change my nation.

When I found I couldn't change the nation, I began to focus on my town.

I couldn't change the town and as an older man, I tried to change my family. Now, as an old man, I realize the only thing I can change is myself, and suddenly I realize that if long ago I had changed myself, I could have made an impact on my family.

My family and I could have made an impact on our town.

Their impact could have changed the nation and I could indeed have changed the world.

UNKNOWN MONK

The Gift

AUTHOR UNKNOWN

Sometimes the most important gifts are given unwittingly. I set about checking the instruments in preparation for my last flight of the day, a short hop from Atlanta to Macon, Georgia. It was 7:30 P.M. Christmas Eve, but instead of forking into Mom's turkey dinner, I was busy getting other people home to their families.

Above the low buzz of talking passengers, I heard a rustle behind me. I looked over my shoulder. Just outside the cockpit doorway was a fresh-faced boy of about nine gazing intently at the flight deck. At my glance he started to turn away.

"Hold up," I called. "Come on in here." I had been about his age when I first saw a flight panel lit up like a Christmas tree, and I could hardly wait to get my first pilot's wings. But now that I was twenty-four and first officer at a commuter airline, I wondered if I'd made the right choice. Here I was spending my first Christmas Eve away from home, and what was I accomplishing? How was I making my mark in the world, let alone doing God's work, just hauling people from city to city?

The boy stepped cautiously into the cockpit. "My name's Chad," I said, sticking out my hand.

With a shy smile he put his hand in mine. "I'm Sam." He turned to the empty seat beside me. "Is that for the captain?"

"It sure is and that's where Captain Jim sits." I patted the worn fabric. "Would you like to try it out?"

Sam blinked at me from under his ball cap. "I don't know...I mean...well, sure, if it's okay." I lowered the seat so he could slide into it. The captain loved to give demonstrations of the plane's gadgets to kids, but what would he think about one sitting in his seat? *Well, it's Christmas,* I thought.

I glanced out at the luggage carts being wheeled toward the plane, thinking of the gifts I wouldn't be able to give in person to my parents and friends the next day. Sam told me he and his family had flown in from Memphis. I checked my watch. The captain would be in any minute, but Sam looked so thrilled, I didn't want to cut short his fun. I gave the instrument panel another once-over, telling Sam what each button and lever did.

Finally Captain Jim clambered aboard. "Howdy, partner." He gave Sam a broad grin. "You know, son," he drawled, "I don't mind you staying with us for a while if you'll switch with me." Sam let the captain take his place and I made introductions.

We began previewing the startup checklist. I kept thinking the captain would send Sam away, but the boy was still peering over my shoulder when the ramp agent radioed to ask if we were ready to turn on the first engine in start sequence, number four.

I relayed the question to the captain, who was studying the weather reports. "I'm still going over these," he said. "You guys go ahead and start it."

"Okay, starting..." I said, positioning the switches. Then I did a double take. "Did you say 'you guys'?"

"Yeah, go ahead."

I looked over at the captain and back at the flight panel. "Right." I flicked on the plane's flashing red beacon to signal the start. Then I turned to my new assistant. "You ever start an airplane before, Sam?"

Eyes wide, he shook his head. Following my instructions, Sam carefully turned a knob on the overhead console that switched on the igniters. Then he pressed a button as big as his hand to start the engine.

Finally, with both hands he slid forward a lever to introduce the fuel. The engine hummed to life.

Sam slowly let go of the lever and stepped back, awestruck. He'd gotten to start an airplane, an honest-to-goodness airliner. I'm not sure if I'd have believed it myself at his age. I thanked Sam for helping us out.

"No, thank you, sir," Sam said. "This was really great!"

As he backed out of the doorway into the cabin, the plane resonated with the sound of the engine he'd started. "You have a merry Christmas, son, you hear?" the captain said.

Sam looked like he was about to cry with happiness.

"I will, sir, I will. Thank you!" With one last look at the flight deck he turned and walked down the aisle. We started up the other engines, took off, and arrived in Macon about forty minutes later.

Early Christmas morning, as we settled into the cockpit for the trip back to Atlanta, one of the gate agents ducked in. "Hey, guys, some kid's mother came by this morning. She wanted to make sure I thanked you for showing her son around last night. Said he couldn't stop talking about the cockpit. She left this for you." The gate agent set a red tin on the center console.

"Well, I'll be," the captain said. He bit into one of the chocolate chip cookies from the tin. Then he unfolded the note taped to its cover and read it silently. He sighed deeply and turned to me. "Boy's got cancer," he said, and read the note aloud:

> Dear Sirs,
>
> Thank you for allowing Sam to watch you work on Christmas Eve night. Sam has cancer and has been undergoing chemotherapy in Memphis. This is the first time he has been home since the treatment began. We drove Sam up to the hospital, but since he loves airplanes, we decided to fly him back home. I am not sure if he will ever get to fly again. His doctor has said that Sam may have only a few months left. Sam has always dreamed of becoming an airline pilot. The flight we took from Memphis to Atlanta was exhilarating for him. He wasn't sure flying on one of your "little" air-

planes would be as much fun, but you two gentlemen gave
him the greatest Christmas gift imaginable. For a few short
minutes his dream came true, thanks to you.

I looked out at the runway gleaming before us in the sun. When I turned back to Jim, he was still staring at the note. A flight attendant came in and said the passengers were ready for departure. She stowed the cookies away and we went through the checklist. Then Captain Jim cleared his throat and called out, "Starting number four."

I'd wanted to be home with my loved ones, exchanging gifts for the holidays. But that little boy showed me that sometimes the most important gifts we give are given unwittingly, and the most precious ones we get come from strangers. I can serve God's purpose no matter where I am, as long as I let the spirit that moved me that night guide me always.

My Little Brother

PAUL KLEINSCHMIDT

Growing up with a brother who was seven years older was difficult.

Scott was my idol, and it hurt not to be able to go the places he did or hang out with his friends. I was always the dorky younger brother who tried so hard to just fit in. All I ever wanted was for him to be proud of me.

So, when Scott announced that he was going to work the summer teaching mentally challenged kids and asked if I'd like to volunteer, I jumped at the chance to spend the time with him.

I was fourteen and the only volunteer at the program. Everyone else was twenty-one and above, either earning college credits in special education like my brother, or trying to make a few bucks for the summer. We had approximately thirty students, ranging in age from eight to twenty-one, with the majority being my age. I had never had much exposure to the world of the mentally challenged and was a bit taken aback on my first day.

Wheelchair after wheelchair rolled off the bus, each with its own special passenger, smiles brighter than the sun in summer. Parents dropping off the bundles of joy, each one filled with the same excitement I felt my first day of school.

And then there was Mikey.

Mikey was nine years old, tall, thin, and severely emotionally disturbed. He stood alone in the corner, waving back and forth, afraid. It was as if he was invisible to all the other students and counselors. I walked over to him, reached out my hand, and he began to scream. I remember the look of embarrassment in my brother's eyes. I wanted to crawl under a rock and just quit. I backed away and tended to the other students.

Every morning Mikey would get dropped off by his mother, and every morning he would go to the same corner where he spent most of his day alone. Even other students would avoid him, not wanting to listen to the screaming or tantrums he would throw.

Each afternoon the counselors would have their students pair off and do different activities. And each afternoon, Mikey would remain in the corner, watching. Feeling more comfortable, I approached the director and asked her about Mikey. She explained that he had been coming to the program for the past couple years, and this was how he spent his days. No one had the time needed to spend with him. I asked her if I could be assigned to him. She didn't respond at first, and I could see the whole you-are-only-fourteen-years-old-what-can-you-do? look in her eyes.

"Sure, go ahead. What could it hurt?" she finally replied.

So each morning Mikey would come in, and I would be waiting for him. He would walk over to his corner, and I would tag right along, standing or sitting next to him for hours, not saying a word. He would scream and everyone would look, but I would just stare straight back at them, determined not to quit. This went on for two weeks. I know all the counselors were talking about me to my brother. This was not what I had envisioned my summer to turn into. It was supposed to strengthen the bond between my brother and me, not make it weaker.

Then something happened that changed my life forever. I overslept one morning and my brother had already taken off to work. I jumped on my bike and rushed to the school, embarrassed for oversleeping and worried I would be in trouble.

I walked into the classroom and the room went silent. *Oh no*, I thought.

That's when I heard it. Someone was clapping his or her hands. I shrugged it off as a student just expressing their excitement. Then someone else began clapping. *Another student,* I thought. No, it was one of the counselors. What was going on? Then it erupted. Everyone was clapping. Were they all being sarcastic that I was late?

It was at that moment that I locked eyes with my brother.

He was clapping the loudest out of everyone and smiling at me. I just stood there puzzled until the director of the program approached me and explained that it had to do with Mikey.

Apparently when Mikey arrived that morning and couldn't find me he went around from table to table, counselor to counselor, asking, "Where's Paul? Where's Paul?"

The director informed me that those were the first words Mikey had spoken in the past couple of years. I didn't know what to say.

I could feel my eyes beginning to fill with tears. I looked over to Mikey in his corner and he was smiling, pointing to me and saying, "Paul! Paul! Paul!"

I felt a hand on my shoulder. It was Scott. "This is my little brother," he kept reminding everyone with pride in his voice. It was then I began to cry.

The next year I was hired to be a counselor. I was only fifteen and had to get a worker's permit. I was in charge of my own group of students and had a college girl as my assistant.

As for Mikey, his family moved out West, and I was saddened by the fact that I would never see him again. I hoped that he was all right and thought of him that whole summer.

The last day of the program I received a postcard from California. In barely legible handwriting were the words "Hi Paul." It was from Mikey. I knew he was going to be okay.

The Bus Passenger

=◎=

AUTHOR UNKNOWN

The passengers on the bus watched sympathetically as the attractive young woman with the white cane made her way carefully up the steps. She paid the driver and, using her hands to feel the location of the seats, walked down the aisle and found a seat he'd told her was empty. Then she settled in, placed her briefcase on her lap, and rested her cane against her leg.

It had been a year since Susan, thirty-four, became blind. Due to a medical misdiagnosis she had been rendered sightless, and she was suddenly thrown into a world of darkness, anger, frustration, and self-pity. Once a fiercely independent woman, Susan now felt condemned by this terrible twist of fate to become a powerless, helpless burden on everyone around her. "How could this have happened to me?" she would plead, her heart knotted with anger.

But no matter how much she cried or ranted or prayed, she knew the painful truth—her sight was never going to return. A cloud of depression hung over Susan's once optimistic spirit. Just getting through each day was an exercise in frustration and exhaustion. And all she had to cling to was her husband, Mark.

Mark was an Air Force officer, and he loved Susan with all of his heart.

When she first lost her sight, he watched her sink into despair and was determined to help his wife gain the strength and confidence she needed to become independent again. Mark's military background had trained him well to deal with sensitive situations, and yet he knew this was the most difficult battle he would ever face.

Finally, Susan felt ready to return to her job, but how would she get there? She used to take the bus, but was now too frightened to get around the city by herself. Mark volunteered to drive her to work each day, even though they worked at opposite ends of the city.

At first, this comforted Susan and fulfilled Mark's need to protect his sightless wife who was so insecure about performing the slightest task. Soon, however, Mark realized that this arrangement wasn't working—it was hectic and costly. *Susan is going to have to start taking the bus again,* he admitted to himself. But just the thought of mentioning it to her made him cringe. She was still so fragile, so angry. How would she react?

Just as Mark predicted, Susan was horrified at the idea of taking the bus again. "I'm blind!" she responded bitterly. "How am I supposed to know where I'm going? I feel like you're abandoning me."

Mark's heart broke to hear these words, but he knew what had to be done. He promised Susan that each morning and evening he would ride the bus with her, for as long as it took, until she got the hang of it. And that is exactly what happened.

For two solid weeks, Mark, military uniform and all, accompanied Susan to and from work each day. He taught her how to rely on her other senses, specifically her hearing, to determine where she was and how to adapt to her new environment. He helped her befriend the bus drivers who could watch out for her and save her a seat. He made her laugh, even on those not-so-good days when she would trip exiting the bus or drop her briefcase.

Each morning they made the journey together, and Mark would take a cab back to his office. Although this routine was even more costly and exhausting than the previous one, Mark knew it was only a matter of time before Susan would be able to ride the bus on her own. He believed in her, in the Susan he used to know before she'd lost her sight, who wasn't afraid of any challenge and who would never, ever quit.

Finally, Susan decided that she was ready to try the trip on her own. Monday morning arrived, and before she left, she threw her arms around Mark, her temporary bus riding companion, her husband, and her best friend.

Her eyes filled with tears of gratitude for his loyalty, his patience, his love. She said good-bye, and for the first time, they went their separate ways. Monday, Tuesday, Wednesday, Thursday.... Each day on her own went perfectly, and Susan had never felt better. She was doing it! She was going to work all by herself!

On Friday morning, Susan took the bus to work as usual. As she was paying for her fare to exit the bus, the driver said, "Boy, I sure envy you." Susan wasn't certain if the driver was speaking to her or not. After all, who on earth would ever envy a blind woman who had struggled just to find the courage to live for the past year?

Curious, she asked the driver, "Why do you say that you envy me?"

The driver responded, "It must feel so good to be taken care of and protected like you are."

Susan had no idea what the driver was talking about and asked again, "What do you mean?"

The driver answered, "You know, every morning for the past week, a fine looking gentleman in a military uniform has been standing across the corner watching you when you get off the bus. He makes sure you cross the street safely and he watches until you enter your office building. Then he blows you a kiss, gives you a little salute, and walks away. You are one lucky lady."

Tears of happiness poured down Susan's cheeks. For although she couldn't physically see him, she had always felt Mark's presence. She was lucky, so lucky, for he had given her a gift more powerful than sight, a gift she didn't need to see to believe—the gift of love that can bring light where there had been darkness.

Attitude Check

Remember the blessings in your life.
It's like sprinkling sunshine on a cloudy day.

ALICE GRAY

Attitude Is Everything

FRANCIE K. BALTAZAR

Jerry is the kind of guy you love to meet in the supermarket. He always has a kind word, a funny joke, or, at the very least, a smile. It doesn't take much to bring on that smile. Jerry's happy if all of the wheels on his grocery cart are going in the same direction. If you ask him how he's doing, he's likely to reply, "If I was doing any better I'd be twins!"

Not many restaurant managers have waiters follow them from one franchise to the next, but Jerry does. They love his attitude. A natural motivator, Jerry can tell if you're having a tough day. "Look on the bright side," he'll say. "If the sun's in your eyes, you sneeze more. It's good for you."

One day a friend said, "I don't get it, Jerry. You can't be positive all the time. How do you do it?"

Jerry replied, "Each morning I wake up and say to myself, 'Jerry, you have two choices today. You can choose to be in a good mood, or you can choose to be in a bad mood.' I choose to be in a good mood. Each time something bad happens, I can choose to be a victim, or I can choose to learn from it. I choose to learn from it. Every time someone comes to me complaining, I can choose to accept their complaining, or I can point out the positive side of life. I choose the positive side."

"Yeah, right," the friend protested. "It's not that easy."

"Oh yes, it is," said Jerry. "Life is all about choices. When you cut away all the rest, every situation is a choice. You choose how you react to situations. You choose how people will affect your mood. You choose to be in a good mood or a bad mood. It's your choice how you live life."

One day Jerry left the back door of his restaurant open, not knowing how his theory would be put to the ultimate test.

Three thieves walked through the door that day and held Jerry at gunpoint. While trying to open the safe, his hand, shaking from nervousness, slipped from the combination lock.

The robbers panicked.

And shot him.

Jerry was rushed to the local trauma center. After eighteen hours of surgery and weeks of intensive care, he was released from the hospital with fragments of the bullets still in his body. Later, when his friend asked him how he was doing, Jerry replied, "If I were any better, I'd be twins...wanna see my scars?"

The friend declined, but asked, "Tell me, what went through your mind during the robbery?"

"The first thing that went through my mind was that I should have locked the back door," replied Jerry. "Then, as I lay on the floor, I remembered that I had two choices; I could choose to live or I could choose to die. I chose to live."

"Weren't you scared?" asked the friend.

Yes, Jerry was scared. "But the paramedics were great," he told his friend. "They kept telling me I was going to be fine. But when they wheeled me into the emergency room and I saw the expressions on the faces of the doctors and nurses, I got really scared. In their eyes, I read, 'He's a dead man.' I knew I needed to take action."

"What did you do?"

"Well, there was a big burly nurse shouting questions at me. She asked if I was allergic to anything. I said 'Yes!'"

The doctors and nurses stopped working and looked at him with concerned wrinkles on their foreheads.

Jerry took a deep breath and said loudly, "I'm allergic to bullets!"

Over their laughter Jerry told them, "Operate on me as if I am alive, not dead." And they did.

Today Jerry is still in the restaurant business. Waiters and waitresses still follow him around, basking in his encouragement, learning from his positive words of advice. Jerry will tell you without blinking that he's alive today because of the skills of some doctors, nurses, and paramedics. But by the time you finish talking with him, you'll know that he's also alive because of his amazing attitude.

The inner side of every cloud is bright and shining;
I therefore turn my clouds about
And always wear them inside out.

ELLEN FOWLER

True Courage

KERI SCHULZ
AGE 15

When I was in second grade I had the most wonderful girl in my class. She was not the most pretty or popular one in the class, or the best player at playing dodgeball or soccer. Actually, to society's standards, there was not really anything that special about her. But she was very special to me. She taught me things by being herself that I could never have learned from anyone else.

Suzanne Smith had a rare liver disease. She was born with a defective liver and would die if not for a transplant. As a baby she underwent the surgery to replace her liver. From then on she had to take antirejection drugs so that her little body would accept the liver. She lived a normal life as best as she could. Suzanne's medication caused some side effects. She got ill much more easily than the other kids and had to be very careful to not catch colds from us.

She started attending Trinity Lutheran School as a kindergartner, and from the very first day, enjoyed every minute of it. Her illness didn't make her sad or depressed or afraid of the future. She was enthusiastic about life. I don't ever remember her complaining about her complications, or anything else for that matter. She never let anything get in the way of having fun and making friends. No sickness would stop her from being the best at the hula hoop in the whole second grade. She seemed to have something special that no one else had. She cared about others so much.

She had all the reasons in the world to be sad or angry or depressed but never let it show.

One day as I was playing handball on the playground, I slipped and fell and scraped my knee. Suzanne was the first person to pick me up. She was the kind of girl that would walk you down to the bathroom and help you get cleaned up and feel better even if it took the whole recess. It would have been easy for her to not care and to think that my scraped knee was nothing compared to her problems. And truthfully, it wasn't. But she didn't think like that. She was overflowing with love for everyone she came in contact with.

Suzanne knew very well that she might not live as long as the other kids in her class, but it didn't bother her. She understood and appreciated the blessing of each new morning more than I might ever know, even at such a young age.

As the year went on, Suzanne's health deteriorated. She always said that she was getting better, but we saw that she was getting more and more sick. As her liver failed, she was put on a waiting list for another transplant. She got sicker and weaker until she couldn't come to school anymore. The classroom seemed bland without her shining smile to light up the room.

Waiting for a liver donor was taking too long; Suzanne's situation was too severe. Her mother offered to donate a piece of her liver to Suzanne. They were flown to Omaha, Nebraska, for the special operation.

On the day of the operation Suzanne didn't even seem afraid. As she and her mother were entering the operating room she held her mom's hand and said, "Don't worry, Mommy, even if I don't make it through this operation, you know I'll see you in heaven."

Suzanne Smith survived the initial operation, but two days later some complications occurred and she passed away during her next operation. When I think of true courage, the first thing I think of is Suzanne.

Thank You, Fozzy!

RUSTY FISCHER

She was a horrible waitress. Never got anybody's order right. Always messed something up on the customers' bills so that they had to complain to the manager. There were stains all over her gaudy pink uniform and runs in her stockings, and her bright red, frizzy hair and the long, bumpy nose planted right in the middle of her oval face made her look just like that lovable Muppet, Fozzy the Bear. Only, our Fozzy wasn't quite so lovable.

Or so I thought...

It was Thanksgiving night and no one else wanted to work, so it was just Fozzy and me slinging turkey shavings and ice cream scoops of mashed potatoes to the clusters of senior citizens who stumbled in out of the brisk November cold.

We had never talked much, and tonight was no exception. The diner had already started in with the Christmas carols on the Muzak, and Fozzy sang right along all night. I tried to share her enthusiasm, but I had troubles of my own.

My father's business was in disarray, and he was considering bankruptcy. After their divorce, my mother had moved to an oceanfront condominium way beyond her means. It had been for sale for a year, and no one had even attempted a bite at her ludicrous asking price.

My life felt out of control and I had no one to turn to. With so many troubles of their own, how could I politely remind my parents that they had always offered to help pay for my college tuition. I had been slaving away at the diner for nearly a year now, trying to save up enough for my first semester at the local state university. I was almost there, and then just this morning, my car hadn't started. I soon learned that the entire electrical system was faulty. It would cost over five hundred dollars to fix.

"Five hundred dollars?" I heard someone respond. I blinked my eyes and stared into Fozzy's solemn face. "And just when you were so close to starting college, too. Not a very happy Thanksgiving, is it?"

Had I really said all of my troubles out loud? And had Fozzy actually listened?

But there we were, nestled quietly over two cups of mudlike diner coffee, as the last few customers of the evening wandered out into the miserable cold.

"Thank you," I said humbly, feeling a lump in my throat at having judged Fozzy so badly. "Thank you for listening. I didn't mean to go on like that."

"Well, now," she sighed. "It doesn't sound like there's much listening going on in your house these days. Everybody rushing around with their own problems. Sometimes a friendly ear can change the way you think about things." She was right. Pouring out my troubles, things I hadn't even told my best friends for fear of embarrassment, had left me feeling like I'd just had a restful night's sleep.

"Listen," she said as we finished our side work and clocked out. "I've been trying to sell my old car for weeks. It's in good shape. Now, it's not exactly a babe magnet, but I'm only asking three hundred dollars for it. That's less than it would take to fix your car. Maybe the money you save would round out what you need for tuition."

"And then some," I gasped, leaping at the offer like a little kid. We sat quietly on the way to her apartment, the only two on the bus. Everyone else was busy celebrating the holiday with family and friends. I thought of my mom at her annual gala Thanksgiving dinner party at the country club. And my dad working double-time at his company to try and make things right. Neither of them had even bothered to ask me what I'd be doing for the holiday.

Fozzy's car was an eleven-year-old Honda with just a little rust and nearly new tires. Its paint job was faded and the interior was worn, but it turned over in an instant and purred like a kitten. There were over 100,000 miles on it, but it was in better shape than the car I was planning on having fixed. I couldn't believe my good luck.

"The paperwork's upstairs," said Fozzy. "You wait here and I'll go get it. I'm sure you have big plans for tonight. I wouldn't want to keep you."

I watched sadly as Fozzy's ample backside waddled slowly away from me. She favored one leg, and the soles of her dollar store shoes looked old and worn. The halls of her building were dark and quiet, and I had picked up enough clues so far to determine that Fozzy wasn't exactly walking into a festive apartment tonight either.

It didn't take long to catch up to her. Her smile filled the corridor as we opened her door, and she fumbled through a cheap desk for the car's paperwork. I sat on a threadbare couch and looked around her one bed-room apartment while she searched. The room was clean and cozy. The table was set with a paper tablecloth bearing turkeys and pilgrims. Turkey candles and pilgrim saltshakers rounded out her festive holiday decorations.

"Oh, I'm sorry," I said, seeing the table set for two and getting up. "I didn't realize you were expecting company."

Fozzy smiled sadly, looking at her feeble attempts to bring the holidays into her home. "Oh no," she sighed. "That's just habit. Ever since my husband died six years ago, I can't stand to see a table set for one. I just leave two plates out so people don't go feeling sorry for me.

"I don't even know why I bothered this year," she added, handing me the car's title as I wrote her a check for three hundred dollars. "You don't need to set a table for takeout Chinese food."

I looked around the room at the shabby furniture and homemade curtains. Scattered about were photographs of several young men and women in various celebratory poses: graduations, promotions, and birth-days. Younger versions of Fozzy were standing nearby, smiling proudly. Where were her own children this holiday night?

Just then my stomach rumbled. I'd been too upset all night to even think about food. Now I was suddenly starving.

"Listen," I said, pulling out the wad of ones and fives from my shift at the diner. "I had a pretty good night. Why don't I order us up some takeout so your nice table here doesn't go to waste? My treat. It's the least I can do to thank you for bailing me out like this."

Fozzy couldn't find the phone fast enough.

Later, as Fozzy showed off the interior of the car and its impressive features, most of which no longer worked, I noticed the stains on her uniform and felt an aching in my heart. Her kind and generous gesture had afforded me the opportunity to finally start college on time. Classes would start soon, I would move away from home and, once settled, find a cushy job on campus and start the process of financial aid and student loans.

My long, hard nights of dishing up buttered carrots and creamed spinach were nearly at an end. I wondered how many long, hard years Fozzy would have to work before she could finally retire.

Driving away in my new used car toward a bright future, thanks to the kind acts of a near stranger, I ran over a bump and the faulty glove box door swung open. Inside was a thin envelope. I opened it at a stoplight and then pulled over until my tears dried up and I could see the road again.

"Thank you for the first Thanksgiving I've celebrated in six years," said a quickly scrawled note on cheap stationery. "This isn't much, but it's all the tips I made tonight. Maybe you can buy one of your textbooks on me. Thanks again, Mavis."

Mavis, I thought, finally pulling back onto the road. All those nights together and it was sitting right there on her name tag the whole time: "Mavis." I counted the money in the envelope. There was enough for two textbooks, but there was also just enough for a brand new uniform for Mavis. I couldn't wait to give it to her the next night.

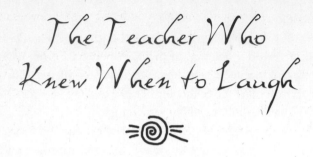

The Teacher Who Knew When to Laugh

MARTI WATSON GARLETT

The boy approaching Walt from down the hall was a slightly built fourteen-year-old wearing tight blue jeans and a black leather jacket, its collar arched near the narrow gold hoop threaded through his ear. His casual, confident attitude proclaimed, "I am in control; I fear no one; don't mess with me."

In contrast to the kid approaching him, Walt wasn't only modest in appearance, he was underwhelming. His shoulders drooped downward, as did his middle, and at the crown of his head was a mass of straight, dark hair that stubbornly resisted his efforts to keep it combed. It stuck out in several ridiculous-looking directions.

Walt knew, via the faculty grapevine, one important fact about the boy approaching him. He knew that this kid was a discipline problem, one tough independent cookie who was not only willing but anxious to frustrate even the best-hearted efforts of good teachers.

On this particular morning, Walt was standing against the wall near the doorway to his classroom. And on this particular morning, Walt had a typical teacher malady.

He had a headache.

In one of his hands was an aspirin. In his other hand was a mug lettered with the words I Are a English Teacher. Inside the mug was a congealing mixture of cold coffee and undissolved powdered creamer. Walt's intent was to pop the aspirin into his mouth and wash it down as quickly as possible.

Meanwhile, the boy strutted nearer. His quick eyes grazed Walt's in one glance, taking in the aspirin and the mug. A private smile slid across his face. His lips barely moved but his words were clear and audible. "Birth control pill, I hope," he said.

Walt had no trouble hearing the comment. The boy made sure of that.

Now Walt had a decision to make. As he saw it, he could deal with the kid in one of three ways. He could grab the smart aleck by the collar and haul him down to the principal's office. Maybe that would wipe the grin off his face and teach him a little respect.

Walt knew this was what the kid was expecting. In fact, he was almost daring Walt to do it.

Walt didn't know him, but Walt suspected the kid's insolence was getting worse, not better. That was the pattern for most discipline problems fed with a regular diet of principal's office.

So Walt considered a second option—ignoring the comment and the kid, looking through and past him as if he didn't exist.

Junior high teachers learn early that discipline problems detest going unnoticed by authority figures. Being noticed is their reason for being.

In Walt's opinion, ignoring a kid, even a discipline problem, was at best spiteful, at worst vengeful. And Walt wasn't comfortable with the idea of teachers wreaking vengeance on their students. So out went option two.

Anyway, Walt didn't like shutting his eyes to things. He liked to give what was in front of him clear-eyed scrutiny. How else could you see what needed fixing?

That left only one more option. Laughing out loud. What, after all, was so offensive about the comment? Actually, Walt thought it was pretty funny.

Doggone it, if the kid had wit, the kid had humor. And if the kid had humor, then the kid didn't take himself too seriously. And if the kid didn't take himself too seriously, maybe he was an all-right kid, a healthy kid.

It was the humorless kid—the humorless *human beings*—who worried Walt. Now *they* were trouble.

Options one and two disappeared; Walt responded with option three—he laughed.

Loudly and appreciatively.

No doubt about it, Walt's laughter was genuine. And so flashed a moment of rapport between Walt and one of this junior high's main discipline problems.

The kid threw Walt an interested look. *Who are you?* The look seemed to ask. *Some sort of real guy or something? You got a sense of humor or something? What gives, man? Aren't you a teacher?*

Meanwhile, Walt was nodding amiably, almost as if he understood every one of the unspoken questions.

"Yeah, birth control pill," Walt finally replied, looking down at the white tablet in his hand. "But, hey, what can I do? It's doctor's orders."

He made a show of placing the aspirin on his tongue. "He told me, my doctor did, he said, 'Walt, how many times do I hafta tell you? You gotta take your pills. Doncha know there're too many of you in the world already?'"

The boy's swagger slowed, and for an instant he looked like a normal adolescent male.

"Too many of you?" the kid said. "Maybe there are"—now his eyes met Walt's directly—"and then again, maybe there aren't."

Wanted:

More to improve and fewer to disapprove.
More doers and fewer talkers.
More to say it can be done
And fewer to say it's impossible.
More to inspire others
And fewer to throw cold water on them.
More to get into the thick of things
And fewer to sit on the sidelines.
More to point out what's right
And fewer to show what's wrong.
More to light a candle
And fewer to curse the darkness.

AUTHOR UNKNOWN

Best Present of All

BONNIE COMPTON HANSON
FROM *HEART STIRRING STORIES OF LOVE*

I quickly scanned the rest of my list. This was already Friday night, and because my weekend was going to be so busy, I was trying to finish my grocery shopping as quickly as possible.

What did I still need? Oh yes, flowers—for we would be visiting my in-laws that weekend for a big dual birthday celebration. Dad was now a young ninety-three; his wife, eighty-three. So after church that Sunday we planned to drive out to their home and take them out for a nice birthday dinner.

After selecting a colorful fall arrangement, I checked my list again. Birthday cards for both of them. Pushing my piled-high cart around to the greeting card aisle, I noticed a young girl there with her mother. It was hard not to. The attractive child was positively glowing with excitement as she held up two gaily colored cards. "Oh, Mom!" she bubbled. "They're both so cool. Can't I get both of them?"

Smiling, the mother shook her head. "No, darling, just one. Hurry and choose the one you want."

"Oh, but I can't choose!" Turning to me, a perfect stranger, she grinned.

"Look—aren't they both just adorable? Which one should I pick?"

I laughed. "Well, dear, that depends on who it's for. Tell me what your friend is like, and I'll give you my recommendation."

She stared at me blankly. "Friend? What friend?"

"Why, the one you're buying the card for, of course."

She giggled. "Oh, my goodness! Didn't you know? The card is for me! See, my birthday's tomorrow. So for my present this year, Mom said I could pick out any card I want all by myself. Isn't that great? OK, Mom, I think I'll take this one." Holding tightly to one card, she put the other one back.

Hardly believing what I'd just heard, I stuttered. "W-why congratulations, dear! How old will you be?"

Hugging her mother, she said, "Eleven."

Tears sprang to my eyes. How could any child—especially an eleven-year-old—get nothing more for her birthday than a two-dollar card?

It just wasn't fair! My first impulse was to reach right into my purse, grab the ten-dollar bill tucked inside, and thrust it into this poor child's hand. After all, I'd be paying for all my own purchases by check, so I didn't really need the cash. Wouldn't that be a loving thing to do?

Then I looked at the embarrassed mother. She was probably a single mom trying desperately to make ends meet. How it would shame her if I did such a thing! So my purse stayed unopened.

"Happy birthday, dear!" I replied instead.

Mother and daughter beamed at each other. Hugging tightly to each other and to the precious card, they hurried off to the checkout stand—having already given to each other the best and most priceless birthday present in the whole world: the gift of love.

Ahh...Life Is Good

DARAH WILSON
AGE 17

Ahh...life is good... Wait, let me take that back. Life is great! I've got my health, my family, a loving mom, stepdad, and brother. I've got friends that care about me, a house to go home to, a room of my own, a warm bed, a dog and two cats, and our refrigerator is full—most of the time. Yep, life is great, but let me tell you...life is not so great for everyone in this world.

It was four years ago that I learned firsthand what life can really be like. A challenge was raised to the teens at my church to build a house for a homeless family in Mexico. At first, it seemed like an impossible, even crazy, idea. Organizing anything with a handful of teenagers can be a hassle, to say the least. But ten teens came forward and accepted the challenge. Most of us had never touched a hammer before, but here we were, headed to the slums of Mexico to build a house for a family of strangers.

For me, it was both exciting and terrifying. But then, I thought back to only two years earlier, when my dad died suddenly from cancer. The thought of living without him had been so overwhelming. But friends and even strangers had reached out to me when I needed it most. I decided that going on this trip was my opportunity to give back.

Our first bus ride across the border from Texas to Mexico started out with laughter and singing. But when we turned onto the dirt road heading into the "colonia" where we would be building, I was totally unprepared for what I saw. Entire families were living in shelters made out of scraps of wood and metal. There was no electricity or running water. Honestly, you could have heard a pin drop as we looked out at poverty we had never seen, or even imagined, before. The home that we built was twelve by sixteen feet, smaller than any one room in my house. It had two windows, a door with a hook. We added a linoleum floor as an extra treat. To all of us here, it would be sufficient as a lawn mower shack but to this one family, it was a palace.

We were there to build and also to reach out to the local children. Every day when we stepped off the bus we were greeted by little kids that lived in the colonia. I was surprised at first at how happy they all seemed. I looked around at the shacks that they lived in and their bare feet on the dirt road, and despite all this, they somehow seemed content. I learned over the course of that one week that these children were very different than any child that I had ever gotten to know in the U.S. Not many of the Mexican kids had any toys to play with, and yet they were all very giving. The few things that they had they wanted to share with us.

Two children stand out in my mind, and I will never forget them. Maria was a little girl and all she owned was a bottle of nail polish, just one little bottle of orange nail polish. She had probably rationed it so that it would last as long as possible, but when we arrived, she insisted on painting all of our fingernails. Bruno was a little boy. I always saw him playing with a rubber bouncy ball. Now, you might be thinking, "Well, a bouncy ball is a nice toy to play with," but his was only half inflated. It had a hole in it and no longer bounced, but this didn't seem to phase him at all. He still played with that ball every day. Not only did he play with it, he did it with a smile on his face. With most of the children that I know and even myself as a little kid, that ball would have been in the trash a long time before.

These two children and others in the colonia participated in a vacation Bible school that I helped out with. We met in the only part of the neighborhood that offered any shade from the hot Mexican sun, under a great big tree. As a part of the program, I was chosen to share the story of my faith. My father's death had played a major role in my faith so I knew

I would have to talk about that. I remember how nervous I was. Not only was it a sensitive subject, but I was also concerned that what I had to share wouldn't be conveyed clearly. Not knowing a word of Spanish, every word I said had to be translated. I hoped and prayed that those listening would understand my message, which was that, despite difficult times, their faith could carry them through.

Afterward, with tears running down my face, the children, to my amazement, gathered around me, hugged me, and showed me a kind of love that I had never felt before. It really struck me that what I was sharing was to benefit them, but they, too, were reaching out to me. I realized then that it didn't matter that we did not speak the same language. I learned that day that the language of love is, truly, universal and can be shared between people of all nationalities.

Choosing to go on that mission trip has been one of the best decisions I've ever made. My time spent in Mexico has been incredible. I have developed a stronger faith of my own—all while helping those in need. I now see the world beyond my immediate surroundings. Things that I otherwise would take for granted, I now cherish. I realize my capabilities to make a difference in this world and the absolute need for me to do so.

The conditions that these people in Mexico live in are horrendous, yet they share their love and happiness despite it all. This coming summer will be my fifth year participating in a mission trip. The things that I have learned and experienced on these trips have molded me into a stronger, more self-confident person and have helped me to cope with many hardships in my life.

When I lost my dad, I experienced firsthand love and compassion from strangers. Mexico has allowed me to give that back. For that, I'll be forever grateful. Life really is great!

Homeless Man?

AUTHOR UNKNOWN

t was a cold winter's day that Sunday. The parking lot to the church was filling up quickly. I noticed as I got out of my car that fellow church members were whispering among themselves as they walked to the church. As I got closer I saw a man leaned up against the wall outside the church. He was almost lying down as if he were asleep. He had on a long trench coat that was almost in shreds and a hat topped his head, pulled down so you could not see his face. He wore shoes that looked thirty years old, too small for his feet, with holes all over them, and his toes stuck out. I assumed this man was homeless, and asleep, so I walked on by through the doors of the church.

We all fellowshipped for a few minutes, and someone brought up the man lying outside. People snickered and gossiped, but no one bothered to ask him to come in, including me. A few moments later church began. We all waited for the preacher to take his place up front, when the doors to the church opened. In came the homeless man walking down the aisle with his head down. People gasped and whispered and made faces. He made his way down the aisle and up to the pulpit where he took off his hat and coat. My heart sank. There stood our preacher...he was the "homeless man." No one said a word. The preacher took his Bible and laid it on the stand. "Folks, I don't think I have to tell you what I am preaching about today...."

Like Geese Flying South

ALAN CLIBURN

Grandpa was raking leaves when Eric turned the corner and hurried up Chestnut Lane. Just seeing his grandfather made Eric feel a little better, and he quickened his pace slightly.

"Hi, Grandpa," he said a moment later, entering the yard.

"I'm glad to see you, Eric," his grandfather said, leading the way to an old-fashioned porch swing.

At least somebody wants me around, Eric thought, bitterly recalling what had happened at the park less than fifteen minutes earlier. But he forced a smile. "Thanks, Grandpa."

"Would you believe that Grandma would rather stay inside working on a quilt than watching the geese fly overhead?"

Eric looked upward to see a giant "V" passing above, made up entirely of geese.

"That's hard to believe, all right," Eric agreed, grinning. He observed the birds as they continued on, maintaining their perfect formation, one of them the undisputed leader. His grin faded as quickly as it had come. Eric knew that feeling of being a leader; he had always been one.

Even when they moved and he was new in the neighborhood, Eric soon had the other boys playing the games he wanted to play and asking for his help to build things. He just always knew how to take charge.

His leadership ability extended into other areas, too. Due to a budget cut, after-school sports had been eliminated at the junior high Eric attended. "Well, good-bye to football," one of the guys muttered when the coach announced the cutback.

"Yeah," somebody else agreed.

"Wait a minute, you guys," Eric began when the coach had finished. "If we want to play football after school, we don't have to do it here. Let's meet at the park at 3:30. I'll bring the football."

Enough guys for two teams showed up for practice at 3:30, so they spent the rest of the afternoon running plays and having a great time. Eric had grinned to himself. *And I set this up,* he thought, satisfied.

Everything was going okay until "he" showed up, Eric thought grimly, remembering the afternoon a tall boy with dark hair and long arms had suddenly appeared. For a few minutes he just stood on the sidelines watching.

"Hey, can I play?" he asked finally.

The other boys looked at Eric, as usual.

"Sure," Eric decided, "go out for a pass."

He threw the ball as hard and as far as he could, but somehow the new guy was there in time to catch it. Then he sent it back, the ball spiraling beautifully as it went straight to Eric.

"What a pass!" one of the guys standing near Eric exclaimed.

At first, Eric was glad to have someone like David on the team, but that feeling was quickly replaced by one of apprehension and uncertainty when the other guys started looking to David for advice. He was more than willing to give it, too. Some of the plays he suggested were pretty good, Eric admitted.

"My dad's the new football coach at State University," David explained when someone asked how come he knew so much about the game. "I've been playing football all my life. I think I had a football in my crib instead of a rattle!"

Everybody laughed, even Eric. But it had been a forced laugh for him. The guys were getting better, there was no doubt about that, but he always hoped and prayed that David wouldn't show up for practice. Oh, he was still the leader—until David arrived. David even brought extra footballs for the guys to practice with when they weren't running plays.

Eric hadn't liked it, but he had been willing to live with it—up until this afternoon.

They were getting ready to run a few plays when the park director arrived on the scene with a clipboard in his hands.

"Listen, I've been watching you guys lately, and I think you're ready for a little competition," he said. "The director of Northside Park thinks he has a pretty tough team, but I told him I had a team over here that's twice as tough. How about this Saturday afternoon at two? Right here."

"That would be great," Eric replied quickly. "Okay with you guys?"

They all nodded agreement.

"We'll have to put together some sort of roster," the park director went on. "Who's the captain of this team?"

"We've never picked one," Eric answered.

"Maybe we'd better do that right now then," the park director decided.

"I nominate David," a voice said.

"I second it," another added.

The voting had been practically unanimous, Eric thought, looking up as more geese flew over. Only a few of his really loyal friends had voted for him. Angry and hurt, he had slipped away when no one was looking, with no plans to return.

"Here's some hot chocolate," his grandfather said, handing a cup to Eric. "My, those geese have been flying south all day. Remember when you used to cry out 'V!' when you saw the geese?"

"No, not really," Eric said. "How do they know to fly in that 'V' formation?"

"I used to think it was just instinct," his grandfather replied, "and to some extent, it is. But it's also aeronautically sound. By flying in a 'V' formation, they somehow encounter less friction and make the trip much faster. Teamwork has a lot to do with it, too. If each bird set out by itself, a lot of them wouldn't make it."

Eric didn't answer. At that moment he didn't appreciate hearing about teamwork.

"And see that bird at the very front?" Grandpa asked.

"Sure," Eric answered, "he's the leader."

"One of the leaders," his grandfather corrected.

Eric frowned. "One of the leaders? There's only room for one bird in the lead position. See?"

"One at a time," his grandfather said. "But when you've watched geese fly south for as many years as I have, you'll discover that pretty soon the lead bird drops back and another one takes its place."

Eric looked up again just as the lead bird in the formation passing overhead did indeed drop back.

"One bird could never stand the strain of leading the formation all the way south," Grandpa continued. "There's a time to lead and a time to rest. Every leader must be a follower sooner or later."

Eric glanced at his grandfather quickly. Did he know what had happened at the park? But the old man was gazing at the sky, obviously enjoying the migration of the geese.

Is that it? Eric wondered. *Had he been a leader so long that he didn't know how to be a follower?* He wouldn't even admit to himself that David was a better football player. Or at least he hadn't admitted it up to now.

"I'd better get back to the park, Grandpa," he said suddenly, standing up. "We have a football game Saturday at two o'clock. Want to come?"

"Wouldn't miss it," his grandfather replied, smiling. "See you then."

Geese flying south for the winter, Eric thought as he hurried back to the park. *God could use anything to teach a guy a lesson!*

Blind Date

YITTA HALBERSTAM AND JUDITH LEVENTHAL
FROM *SMALL MIRACLES*

*S*he had felt an immediate kinship with him and thought the feeling was mutual.

He had taken an instant dislike to her and couldn't wait to take her back home.

The hours flew by for *her;* time had never seemed to pass so quickly. To *him,* every minute was an eternity.

She wished the night would never end.

He was sorry it had ever begun. Still, he was a gentleman and he didn't want to hurt her feelings. She was, after all, sweet and soft and kind—just not his type. He was attracted to women who were mysterious and aloof, confident and smug. The kind of women who never went out on blind dates set up by anxious friends.

When he had called her on Monday, he had detailed his plans for the Saturday night date, seeking her approval. Dinner, a Broadway show, dancing at the new club everyone was raving about. He couldn't back out of it now; it would be too much of a rebuff.

Her eyes lit up with joy as the evening stretched out before them; *his* glazed over with boredom.

Then the date was finally over. *She* sighed, Too bad; *he* breathed, Thank goodness! He drove her back to her home in Brooklyn and eagerly pushed the door handle on the driver's side so he could escort her inside.

There was one minor problem.

The car door was jammed.

"That's weird," he muttered, consternation flooding his face as he tried to jimmy the handle open.

It wouldn't budge.

He banged the door with his fist, kicked it with his foot, shoved it with his shoulder. To no avail. It was absolutely, positively, and very mysteriously, stuck.

Flustered, he turned to her with his apologies.

"Sorry," he said, "but we'll have to go out through the door on your side. Do you mind?"

She tugged at the handle, and he waited for the door to swing wide open, offering deliverance and escape.

Her door wouldn't budge, either.

"This is so bizarre!" he exclaimed. "We went in and out of the car at least a half dozen times tonight, and there was nothing wrong with either door. There wasn't even a hint of any problem. I just don't understand it. It's not as if it's icy outside or freezing. Why should the doors jam right now?"

The car was a two-door model. It was the middle of the night, and they were in the middle of a very quiet, middle-class Brooklyn neighborhood. The houses lining the block were dark; none blazed with light or life. Not a single soul seemed to be stirring on the sleepy, deserted street. It was in the days before cell phones, and as frantic for flight as he was, he knew it would be cruel and unfair to use his horn to signal trouble and wake up the sleeping residents. Deliverance from his date might have to be postponed awhile.

"Well," he said, turning to her with a rueful smile, "I guess we'll just have to wait until someone drives by and rescues us.... I'm sure there are other young people on the block who stay out late on Saturday night."

"I don't know..." she said hesitantly. "Most of the people living on this street are pretty elderly."

Inwardly, he shuddered. Outwardly, he flashed her a dazzlingly false grin that in her naivete she took to be genuine.

"But hey," she said, brightening at the prospect of spending more time with him, "we can get a chance to truly talk now.... The show and the dancing were great, but they didn't give us much time to really get to know each other.... So tell me," she said, turning to him with an open, interested smile, "what do you think of...?"

Better make the best of it, he groaned, resigning himself to a few hours of boredom. But as she drew him into the conversation, he found himself increasingly enchanted by her candor, her little enthusiasms, her vivacity. She was intelligent, well-read, easygoing. And she was, to be fair, a really good sport about the jammed doors. Maybe he had misjudged her. Maybe it had been unfair to dismiss her so quickly. Maybe first impressions weren't the right impressions, after all. Maybe he would even ask her out...again.

It's been ten years since that fateful night and they've been happily married for the last nine and a half.

They never could figure out why the car doors jammed that night, but actually, in retrospect, they're glad they did.

I will go pick daisies and have a happy heart.

KIMBER ANNIE ENGSTROM

A New Creation

CHRISTINA THUERWACHTER
AGE 16

The butterfly flapped its wings, exposing a myriad of brilliant colors. Golden specks shimmered in the blazing sunlight. Gracefully, it fluttered up into the vast blue sky, soaring freely in the gentle breeze.

I was amazed as I observed this stunning creature. It began as nothing but a brown, sluggish caterpillar. Now it had been transformed into a whole new creation. It was now a beautiful butterfly with ravishing wings to fly.

I was reminded of myself and my own journey through transformation. Months ago, I was walking around dead inside. I had been battling with anorexia for four years. I used my eating disorder as an escape, a way to deaden the hurt inside of me. Over the years, it had slowly begun to kill me.

I was occupied with this obsession, this nightmare that would not end. Day after day, food was my only focus. I felt worthless, ugly, and fat. I felt life wasn't worth living. I just wanted to shrink away to nothing.

My family and friends were greatly concerned. My doctors were at their wits' end trying to help me. I was hospitalized several times, but to no avail. I just kept creeping deeper and deeper into anorexia, distancing myself from the world.

Eventually, I received the help I so desperately needed. I was sent to a treatment center in Arizona. It became my cocoon, where I slowly began my journey toward transformation. An eating disorder does not change overnight; it takes hard work and persistence. However, I learned to accept myself and believe in myself. Most importantly, I learned that God loves me just the way I am.

I broke out of my cocoon, a new creation. God gave me wings to soar, and I believe I can fly.

Start by doing what's necessary,
then what's possible
and suddenly you are doing the impossible.

ST. FRANCIS OF ASSISI

You Know What's Right

Happiness comes to those who are fair to others and are always just and good.

PSALM 106:3

THE LIVING BIBLE

The Pre-Dawn Test

ELAINE CUNNINGHAM

R-r-r-ing. *Is that the doorbell? I looked at the clock. Five-thirty. Who could be ringing our doorbell this early?*

My husband rolled out of bed and went to the front door. I heard a mumble of voices, and then he returned.

"Honey, could you get up and help me? A homeless man needs some breakfast."

I groaned. Since my husband was a pastor this was not the first time I'd been called to help a needy person on our doorstep, but it was a bit inconvenient this morning. Not only was it black as night outside, I knew our refrigerator looked like Mother Hubbard's cupboard. "It's a poor time to feed anyone. You know we're moving next week. I've cleaned out the fridge and most of the cupboards."

"Well, see what you can find. He looks desperate."

I scrambled out of bed, threw on my bathrobe, and headed for the kitchen.

There, in a chair in the corner, sat the most pitiful piece of humanity I'd seen in years. A tattered felt hat hid his eyes. An old scarf covered the rest of his face. His long, ragged coat dragged to the floor.

"Would you like to take off your coat?" I asked.

"No," he mumbled through the scarf. His body shook. "I'm c-c-cold."

I opened the refrigerator door. *Hmmmm. A few slices of bacon would have to do. Maybe there's an egg left.* I found three. I took a frying pan out of the cupboard and turned on a front burner on the stove. As I opened the package of bacon and peeled off two slices, I glanced again at the man. He still sat bundled up, shaking with cold, or palsy, or something. *Poor old soul. Maybe this is one of "the least" Jesus said we should befriend. You couldn't get much more least than this one.*

I turned back to the stove and laid the limp slices of bacon in the skillet. They sizzled as they hit the hot pan. *This is probably the first good meal this fellow's had in a while.* I prayed for him silently as I concentrated on turning over the bacon slices.

Suddenly, the man in the corner leaped from his chair, ran toward me, and threw his arms around me!

"Mom," he yelled, and tossed off his hat and scarf.

My heart pounded with fright, then relief, then laughter, as I looked into the mischievous eyes of my son who was supposed to be away at college in Kansas City, not posing as a vagabond in Indiana.

"You passed the test, Mom," he said, still embracing me. "I thought I'd surprise you with this disguise to see if you would feed me early in the morning. I drove all night to get here."

"Well, you certainly surprised me—almost gave me a heart attack. You're lucky I didn't crack you on the head with the frying pan."

Later, after my heart had stopped pounding, I reflected on my son's test and realized what a good reminder it was to be ready to help the needy for Jesus' sake, even at 5:30 A.M. Next time, though, I'll watch closely for a twinkle in the eye—just in case.

2:00 A.M.

D. B.

FROM *SONS: A FATHER'S LOVE*

When I was sixteen and finally had my own car, Dad told me to be in by 12:30. I didn't mind having a curfew—every kid I knew had to be in by a certain time. But when I turned eighteen, I guess I kind of rebelled at the idea. I didn't really feel like talking to Dad about it because I didn't want to argue with him. But one night I stayed over at my friend's house until 2:00 A.M.

When I finally rolled into our driveway, I noticed that the lights were still on in the living room. I tiptoed through the door, but my efforts not to disturb anyone were wasted: Mom and Dad were sitting on the couch together, and Mom was crying.

"What are you guys doing up?" I asked innocently.

"Waiting for you to come home," my father said in a calm voice. "We figured something had happened to you, because you always call if you're going to be late. Are you all right?"

"Of course I'm all right," I retorted defensively. "I'm eighteen years old and I shouldn't have to check in with you like a child. I don't need rules like that, Dad."

"It's not about rule keeping, David. It's about consideration. The only reason we want you to call us is to keep us from worrying. We really thought something had happened to you tonight."

"Yeah, right...well, I'm fine. And I'm here, so let's all go to bed." My voice sounded colder than I meant for it to. "Sorry for the inconvenience," I added, sounding a little too formal for the occasion.

Two weeks later, my folks went out somewhere. They may have told me where they were going, but I wasn't really listening. At midnight, I realized that they weren't home yet. I was working on my car, and I didn't think much about it until 1:00. Then I started wondering where they were. By 1:30 I was feeling uneasy. By 2:00 I was really worried. And by 2:45, I was trying to figure out whether to call the highway patrol or not. I decided to make the call. My hands shook as I picked up the phone, and just as I pushed the 9 in 911, I heard Dad's car pull into the driveway.

Moments later they walked through the door, all dressed up and looking very happy.

"Where have you been?" I roared. "I was just calling the police when you pulled up."

"Why on earth were you calling the police? We were in the city at a play. I told you where we were going."

"You didn't tell me anything! You should have let me know..."

Mom looked sympathetic, but Dad didn't.

"I thought you'd had a wreck or something," I continued, gradually realizing that the tables had been turned.

Dad's face was serious, but he had a telltale twinkle in his eye. "We can come home any time we want," he countered, looking me in the eye.

"Of course you can, but..."

"Now do you understand why it's a good idea to let people know where you are?" Dad squeezed my shoulder. "It's not about curfews, it's about consideration."

I felt something wet on my face and realized my eyes were overflowing with tears. Only then did I understand how scared I had been and just how thoroughly I had learned my lesson.

Donuts at the Back

WAYNE RICE

FROM *STILL MORE HOT ILLUSTRATIONS FOR YOUTH TALKS*

i was holding a notice from my 14-year-old son's school announcing a meeting to review the new course in sexuality. Parents could examine the curriculum and take part in an actual lesson presented exactly as it would be given to the students.

Arriving at the school, I was surprised to discover only about a dozen parents gathered, waiting for the presentation. I picked up a teacher guide and thumbed through page after page of instructions in the prevention of pregnancy or disease. Abstinence was mentioned only in passing.

When the teacher arrived with the school nurse, she asked if there were any questions. I asked why abstinence did not play a noticeable part in the material. What happened next shocked me. Speaking over a great deal of laughter, someone suggested that if I thought abstinence had any merit, I should go back to burying my head in the sand. The teacher and the nurse said nothing as I drowned in a sea of embarrassment. My mind had gone blank, and I could think of nothing to say. The teacher explained to me that the job of the school was to teach facts; the home was responsible for moral training. I sat in silence for the next twenty minutes as she explained the course to parents who seemed to give their unqualified support to the materials.

"Donuts at the back," announced the teacher during the break. "I'd like you to put on the name tags we've prepared—they're right by the donuts—and mingle with the other parents." Everyone moved to the back of the room. As I watched them affixing their name tags and shaking hands, I sat deep in thought. I was ashamed that I had not been able to convince them to include a serious discussion of abstinence in the materials.

I uttered a silent prayer for guidance. My thoughts were interrupted by the teacher's hand on my shoulder. "Won't you join the others, Mr. Daniels?"

The nurse smiled sweetly at me. "The donuts are good."

"Thank you, no," I replied.

"Well then, how about a name tag? I'm sure the others would like to meet you."

"Somehow I doubt that," I replied.

"Won't you please join them?" she coaxed. Then I heard a still, small voice whisper, "Don't go." The instruction was unmistakable. "Don't go!"

"I'll just wait here," I said.

The teacher called the class back to order and, looking around the long table, thanked everyone for putting on name tags. She ignored me. "Now we're going to give you the same lesson we'll be giving your children," she began.

"Everyone, please peel off your name tags." I watched in silence as the tags came off. "Now then, on the back of one of the tags, I drew a tiny flower. Who has it, please?"

The gentleman across from me held it up. "Here it is!"

"All right," she said. "The flower represents disease. Do you recall with whom you shook hands?" He pointed to a couple of people. "Very good," she replied. "The handshake in this case represents intimacy. So the two people you had contact with now have the disease." That produced another round of laughter and witty comments.

"And with whom did the two of you shake hands?" the teacher continued. She had made her point. "This demonstrates for students how quickly disease is spread. Since we all shook hands, we all have the disease."

At that moment I heard again the still, small voice. "Speak now," it said, "but be humble." Noting wryly the latter admonition, I rose from my chair and apologized for any upset I might have caused earlier. I then congratulated the teacher on an excellent lesson that would impress the youth and concluded by saying I had only one small point I wished to make.

"Not all of us were infected," I said. "One of us...abstained."

All it takes for evil to triumph is for good men to do nothing.

EDMUND BURKE

Honesty Still Pays

REBECCA PARK TOTILO

Holding my breath, I tore open the envelope from the federal grants office. The letter read: You qualify to receive $750 in assistance for your college tuition. *Finally!* I thought, breathing a sigh of relief. *I can finish my college degree.*

My volunteer internship with Teen Challenge-Hawaii was almost over. Even the beautiful scenery of black sand beaches and majestic palm trees didn't hold the same excitement I felt as returning to school. Staring at my airline ticket, tears filled my eyes, thinking I would also get a chance to visit my mother for a couple of weeks before starting classes.

Stretched out on the den sofa, I daydreamed about the courses I would take and reviewed the catalogs again for the hundredth time. After reviewing the federal grant criteria again, I learned a student living with their parents for two weeks or more is considered a dependent in determining eligibility. My mother's social security disqualified me from receiving a grant, though she was unable to help me with tuition. Three weeks had passed and I felt convicted to tell on myself.

Maybe if I wrote a letter to my U.S. senator explaining the situation, he would tell me to keep the money, I thought. No such luck. The U.S. senator wrote back a three-page letter, quoting the law regarding receiving federal aid.

When I phoned the university, the person on the other end hastened to say, "So what, just lie about it. Nobody knows you lived with your mother for three weeks." Yet I knew.

I asked to speak to someone else in the financial aid office. The young gentleman on the other end replied, "Why worry about it, everybody lies." I couldn't.

Finally, after speaking to a financial aid officer, she said, "The grant went toward your tuition. You must pay the money back to the government by the first day of school." Classes began in less than a week. My dream of obtaining my college degree faded.

My mind raced, while dodging traffic to the downtown campus. "What other choice do I have?" I whispered to myself. Telling the truth was the only option for me. Passing by the long lines in the bookstore, watching students hustle to finalize last minute details, were only reminders of what I wouldn't be a part of. I trudged up the stairs to the financial aid office and informed the director I would not be accepting the federal grant since I was no longer eligible.

Her jaw dropped, as she shook her head in disbelief. "No one has ever given money back before," she cried.

"I have to be honest," I explained.

She wrapped her arm around my shoulder and led me through the office saying, "You've got to meet this young lady. There are actually still honest people in this world!" No one could believe it.

"Nobody is honest these days," the office workers agreed.

"We're going to help you," the director declared. However, all avenues of financial aid were tapped out. It felt great being patted on the back for being honest, but I went home not knowing where the money would come from.

That night I prayed, "God, I stood up for what is right, so please help me now."

The next day, the financial aid office called and asked me to come down. The director smiled when our eyes met through the glass doors. Handing me an envelope she announced, "This is for you." While office staff looked on, I read a letter from the vice-president of the university.

"Congratulations for your honesty…. It would be a privilege to have you attend our university at the college's expense," he wrote.

The envelope contained a check for $750. I leaped for joy and shouted, "Who says honesty doesn't pay?"

Always do what is right—this will gratify some and astonish the rest.

MARK TWAIN

Important Words

The six most important words: "I admit I made a mistake."
The five most important words: "You did a good job."
The four most important words: "What is your opinion?"
The three most important words: "If you please."
The two most important words: "Thank you."
The most important word: "We."
The least important word: "I."

AUTHOR UNKNOWN

The Ride

KELSIE PATKA
AGE 14

i work at Crystal Peaks Youth Ranch during the summer. I remember one particular day last summer when I was sitting in the shade and saw a lady in a pink tank top walking up the driveway. I could tell that she had been really sick, because by the time she got up to the ranch, she was completely out of breath.

This lady had brought her two kids to the ranch so that they could ride horses. She had come to watch. I was sitting there when she came and sat down beside me.

We had been talking for a while about the ranch when she asked me if she could ride. I knew that she wasn't in the best of shape. She had told me that she had been in and out of several hospitals. It had only been in February that she had been allowed to leave her house and bed. However, something inside of me told me that I should say yes, and I did.

I went down and got the horse, since the lady couldn't walk that far. The only horse left for her to ride was a horse named Lightfoot, a little white Arab. When we finally got him tacked up and ready to go, we had to take a break; she was so tired. As I looked down, I saw she was wearing sandals. You had to ride with boots, so I traded shoes with her, and I wore her sandals.

After about ten minutes we walked up to the arena. People just stopped and watched us go by. They could not believe that this lady who had been so sick was about to ride a horse. Even her husband, who had come up to see their kids ride, had some doubts; he expected that she would give up before we got up to the arena. However, she had told me so sincerely that she was going to ride, that I knew that she would show everyone she could do it.

She got on the horse, and I walked beside her and told her the basics of riding. We walked for a long time. She was on the horse while I was on the ground. Finally she asked if she could trot. I knew that she was not the best rider in the world, but I went over the basics and let her do it. I remember watching her trot on this little white Arab with its gray spots, around and around. Then we went through the basics of cantering.

As I watched her canter I heard her say, "I am flying! Look at me, I am flying!" And everyone stopped and watched her in awe.

After a little while she stopped cantering and walked. I walked beside her and started talking to her. We both agreed that this day was meant to be just for her.

Kim, the lady who owned and ran the ranch, came up. She asked this lady, "Did you know that this horse almost died?" As she asked her, Kim pulled back Lightfoot's mane and showed her a foot-long scar. The lady started to cry, and she pulled down her shirt a little, and there was a huge scar.

"I almost died, too," she said with tears coming down her face. She and Kim hugged and cried for a little while, and then I heard Kim say to her, "...a match made in heaven."

She rode a little longer that day. While she was walking Lightfoot around, Kim and I went into the middle of the arena. As we walked there, Kim looked down at my shoes. I had on these ugly sandals, and my socks were all dirty. She looked up at me, and I looked down at the shoes, and back at her.

I said with a grin, "The rules say you cannot ride without boots, so I gave her my shoes." I knew then that I had changed someone's life there just by giving her my shoes. I knew then that the little things we do in life can change lives.

A Wise Maneuver

CAROLE MAYHALL
FROM *HEARTPRINTS*

"Carole, I'm not going to tell you not to smoke." Mother's brown eyes looked serious as I glanced at her in surprise. A few of my girlfriends had begun to experiment with smoking "behind the barn," and Mother and I were discussing it. I knew my parents disapproved of smoking, so I was quite shocked by her initial statement.

She continued, "I cannot be either your judge or your keeper as you are growing up, so I'm not going to tell you that you must not smoke." She paused and then said, "But I am going to ask you to promise me that you will smoke your first cigarette in front of me."

In our household, a promise was not given lightly. It had the solemnity of a sacred oath sworn on the Bible. To my knowledge my parents had never broken a promise to me, and we were expected to act just as honorably.

A wise woman, my mother. I didn't know it when I promised that day, but she had just taken all the wicked fun out of sneaking off somewhere to smoke with friends. To this day I have never had a cigarette in my lips, because who in her right mind would smoke her first in front of a mother she loved and respected, and whom she knew would be heartbroken to witness the event? Definitely not this kid!

The Emperor's Seeds

WAYNE RICE

FROM *MORE HOT ILLUSTRATIONS FOR YOUTH TALKS*

Once there was an emperor in the Far East who was growing old and knew the time was coming to choose his successor. Instead of choosing one of his assistants or one of his own children, he decided to do something different.

He called all the young people in the kingdom together one day. He said, "It has come time for me to step down and to choose the next emperor. I have decided to choose one of you." The kids were shocked! But the emperor continued. "I am going to give each one of you a seed today. One seed. It is a very special seed. I want you to go home, plant the seed, water it, and come back here one year from today with what you have grown from this one seed. I will then judge the plants that you bring to me, and the one I choose will be the next emperor of the kingdom!"

There was one boy named Ling who was there that day and he, like the others, received a seed. He went home and excitedly told his mother the whole story. She helped him get a pot and some planting soil, and he planted the seed and watered it carefully. Every day he would water it and watch to see if it had grown.

After about three weeks, some of the other youths began to talk about their seeds and the plants that were beginning to grow. Ling kept going home and checking his seed, but nothing ever grew. Three weeks, four weeks, five weeks went by. Still nothing.

By now others were talking about their plants but Ling didn't have a plant, and he felt like a failure. Six months went by, still nothing in Ling's pot. He just knew he had killed his seed. Everyone else had trees and small plants, but he had nothing. Ling didn't say anything to his friends, however. He just kept waiting for his seed to grow.

A year finally went by and all the youths of the kingdom brought their plants to the emperor for inspection. Ling told his mother that he wasn't going to take an empty pot. But she encouraged him to go, and to take his pot, and to be honest about what happened. Ling felt sick to his stomach, but he knew his mother was right. He took his empty pot to the palace.

When Ling arrived, he was amazed at the variety of plants grown by all the other youths. They were beautiful, in all shapes and sizes. Ling put his empty pot on the floor and many of the other kids laughed at him. A few felt sorry for him and just said, "Hey, nice try."

When the emperor arrived, he surveyed the room and greeted the young people. Ling just tried to hide in the back. "My, what great plants, trees and flowers you have grown," said the emperor. "Today, one of you will be appointed the next emperor!"

All of a sudden, the emperor spotted Ling at the back of the room with his empty pot. He ordered his guards to bring him to the front.

Ling was terrified. "The emperor knows I'm a failure! Maybe he will have me killed!"

When Ling got to the front, the emperor asked his name. "My name is Ling," he replied. All the kids were laughing and making fun of him. The emperor asked everyone to quiet down. He looked at Ling, and then announced to the crowd, "Behold your new emperor! His name is Ling!"

Ling couldn't believe it. Ling couldn't even grow his seed. How could he be the new emperor?

Then the emperor said, "One year ago today, I gave everyone here a seed. I told you to take the seed, plant it, water it, and bring it back to me today. But I gave you all boiled seeds which would not grow. All of you, except Ling, have brought me trees and plants and flowers. When you found that the seed would not grow, you substituted another seed for the one I gave you. Ling was the only one with the courage and honesty to bring me a pot with my seed in it. Therefore, he is the one who will be the new emperor!"

Kind words can be short and easy to speak,
but their echoes are truly endless.

MOTHER TERESA

Character in Action

BARBARA A. LEWIS
FROM *WHAT DO YOU STAND FOR?*

*J*ana Benally grew to be five feet eleven inches—and a star on her high school volleyball team. She spiked, blocked, and scooped up impossible smashes from the other team before they hit the floor. Her team members trusted her skills and depended upon her honesty.

But Jana hadn't always been completely honest. When she was in the fourth grade, she lied to her teacher when he asked her if she were chewing gum. "I quickly swallowed the gum and said 'No,'" Jana remembers. "The dumb thing about it was that I didn't need to lie. He probably would have just asked me to spit it out. I felt so guilty, I couldn't think about anything else, and I vowed I would never lie again."

But she did lie again, and she cheated, too. "In fifth grade, my friends and I had a huge social studies assignment. We were all good students and liked to finish our assignments ahead of time. So we divided up the parts and copied from each other." Then her teacher, who conducted secret raids on her students' desks, found three of their notebooks in one desk, all with the same answers. The teacher called in the girls and their parents for a talk.

When Jana and her parents went to see her teacher, Jana's stomach dropped, and all she could see were her teacher's big, round, horrified eyes, with eyelashes that poked straight up as if they were drawn on her eyelids. Jana burst into tears and confessed. This time, she promised herself that she would never cheat again—or lie. For real.

And she didn't, even under pressure. Tremendous pressure. When she was a sophomore at San Juan High School, her team played Morgan High School in the state volleyball championship. The game was tight. Morgan would score, then San Juan would score. Jana leaped, dove, smashed the ball, and wiped the sweat from her forehead between plays.

Near the end of the game, the score was 12 to 14, with Morgan ahead. Morgan only needed one more point to win the state championship. Morgan served to San Juan, and Jana's team passed the ball to the center. Jana set it up and spiked it down hard on Morgan's side of the net. A Morgan player dove for the ball and miraculously dug it up from the back row. The Morgan setter went underneath it and set the ball up to the offhand hitter, who spiked it to San Juan. Jana blocked the ball and it smashed down, in-bounds, on Morgan's side.

The referee blew his whistle and yelled "Side out!" San Juan got the ball, and Jana knew that her team could tie the game and maybe even win. But there was just one problem. As Jana had blocked the spike from Morgan, she had felt the underside of her arm brush the net. The referee hadn't seen it. Nobody knew but Jana.

She hesitated for a moment. Then she grabbed the net, motioned to the referee, and said, "I touched the net."

Jana's coach glowered and shouted at her. "Let the ref call the game!"

The referee called "Time out!" As he studied Jana's face, his eyes widened into circles. He paused. Then he blew the whistle, called the net ball, and gave the point to Morgan.

Jana took a long, scorching shower before she left the locker room. It was quiet. Her shoes squeaked as she crossed the empty gym floor. No one on her team had blamed her—but they hadn't congratulated her for being honest, either. No one had said much of anything to Jana after the game. But she knew that it took a whole team to win or lose, and she didn't blame herself, either. Although the state championship was blown away, Jana smiled, because inside she knew she had really won.

My First Job

TONY HILLERMAN
FROM *READER'S DIGEST*

I was fourteen when Mr. Ingram knocked on our farmhouse door in Sacred Heart, Oklahoma (population 38). The old sharecropper lived about a mile down the road and needed help mowing an alfalfa field. It was the first time I was actually paid for work—about twelve cents an hour, not bad when you consider it was 1939 and we were still mired in the Great Depression.

Mr. Ingram liked the job I did and ended up hiring me to dig postholes. I even helped to deliver a calf. One day he found an old truck that was stuck in the soft, sandy soil of the melon patch. It was loaded up with melons that someone had tried to steal before their truck got bogged down.

Mr. Ingram explained that the truck's owner would be returning soon, and he wanted me to watch and learn. It wasn't long before a local guy with a terrible reputation for fighting and stealing showed up with his two full-grown sons. They looked really angry.

Calmly Mr. Ingram said, "Well, I see you was wantin' to buy some watermelons."

There was a long silence before the man answered, "Yeah, I guess so. What are you gettin' for 'em?"

"Twenty-five cents each."

"Well, I guess that would be fair enough if you help me get my truck out of here."

It turned out to be our biggest sale of the summer, and a nasty, perhaps violent, incident had been avoided. After they left, Mr. Ingram smiled and said to me, "Son, if you don't forgive your enemies, you're going to run out of friends."

Mr. Ingram died a few years later, but I have never forgotten him or what he taught me on my first job.

*No one is ever stronger
and stands higher
than when he forgives.*

AUTHOR UNKNOWN

Forward

CHRISTINA M. ABT

Have you ever had "one of those days" where no matter how hard you try, nothing goes right?

Well, Melissa Fortin is a veteran of those kinds of days. In fact, you might say that the twenty-seven-year-old western New York native has been having "one of those years," as she has been juggling a demanding two-job lifestyle in a struggle to make ends meet.

Just last week Melissa received an overdue notice on her car loan. The note demanded not only the late payment, but also the following month's installment. A grand total of five hundred and thirty-eight dollars due.

Melissa honestly admits, "I just couldn't pay it all so I wrote a check for half the amount and put it aside to mail." But a funny thing happened on the way to the post office. While running an errand at a local department store, Melissa lost the payment.

"Apparently, when I pulled my car keys out of my purse, the envelope fell out." A loss undetected until the young woman's arrival at the post office.

Immediately, she retraced her steps. "I searched the parking lot and the store. I even left my name at the desk in case someone found it."

Which is exactly what happened.

That night, Melissa's phone rang.

"This woman called and said she found my envelope in the parking lot and put a stamp on it and mailed it. I was a little floored and didn't know whether to believe her. But I was so relieved that I just thanked her and hung up. I didn't even think to ask her name. I just assumed she worked at the department store."

But that's not where this story ends.

Two days later, Melissa received a letter in her mailbox. The address: typewritten. The postmark: local. The return address: blank. Inside: a note of kindness unlike any the young woman had ever read, written by the individual who found her car payment.

The author explained that since there was no return address on Melissa's payment, she and her husband had decided to open it for identification purposes. Upon closer inspection, the couple realized that the payment was incomplete. So they decided to include a check of their own to cover the balance. That's right. This couple paid $269.02 on an installment loan for a person they had never met, on a car they didn't own.

They explained their motivation for the charitable act with a simple three-word phrase: Pay it forward.

It seems that several days earlier, the couple attended a screening of the Helen Hunt, Kevin Spacey movie of the same name. Like many theatergoers they became entranced with the film's concept of doing for others, simply for the promise of inspiring like actions. As in the movie, the benefactors requested that Melissa "forward" some form of their good deed to three others that she judged to be in need. They anonymously closed the letter with an endearing, "Your friends."

Melissa's reaction?

"I was overwhelmed. I wasn't sure whether to believe it. But then I called the loan company, and their records showed the entire payment was made." After sharing her story with family and friends, Melissa told her tale to a local newspaper. The story ran on the front page of the *Buffalo News* complete with a color picture of this fortuitously smiling brown-haired beauty. Within days, newspapers in downstate New York, New Jersey, Tennessee, and Oregon featured her account. Television and radio interviews followed. Her phone rang off the hook. People stopped her at work. Everyone was anxious to share in Melissa's "pay it forward" phenomena.

But more significant to Melissa than the notoriety is the personal impact of the deed.

"This is one of the best things that has ever happened to me. And I believe that this will change the outcome of my life. I definitely know it has changed me to think more about the way I act and think, about everything."

Regarding the hope of someday meeting "her friends," Melissa is acceptingly philosophic.

"I thought they might contact me, but I guess they're not going to call. I just hope they saw the television piece or read the newspaper article and know how thankful I am."

As for the million dollar question…will she pay it forward?

"Definitely. And I hope when I do, it inspires other people to do the same."

And so on, and so on, and so on….

After the verb "To Love," "To Help" is the most beautiful word in the world.

ROBERT LOUIS STEVENSON

The Flat Tire

WAYNE RICE

FROM *STILL MORE HOT ILLUSTRATIONS FOR YOUTH TALKS*

Two students were taking organic chemistry at the university. Having done well in their work and labs, they were both going into the final exam with solid A's. So far so good. Trouble was, they were so confident that they decided to party the night before the big test. It was a great night; one thing led to another, and they ended up sleeping late the following morning.

They missed the exam! Disasterville! Being inventive souls, though, they went to see the professor to explain that they had been visiting a sick, out-of-town friend the night before. On the way home they had a flat tire. With no spare tire and no car jack, they were stranded. They could only manage to hitch a lift back to town midmorning, which is why they missed the test. They were really sorry to have missed the exam, they said (they were so looking forward to it!), but wondered whether they might be able to take it that afternoon.

The professor thought about it for a moment and decided that this would be permissible, since they hadn't had time to discuss the exam with any of the students who had already taken it. After a short break for lunch, the two students were ready for the test. The professor placed them in separate rooms, handed each of them an exam booklet, and told them to begin.

Page one, question one. A simple one for five points. This will be easy! Having answered the first question each of the students turned the page for question number two:

It read: "Which tire?" (95 points).

Hang in There

Keep your face to the sunshine
and you cannot see the shadow.

HELEN KELLER

Ed's Closet

ROBIN MAYNARD

When I was eleven years old and my brother was five, our parents decided to divorce. We were young and didn't understand what divorce meant and how it would actually affect us. A few days later, it became very clear. Our father announced that he was moving twelve hundred miles away to Tulsa, Oklahoma. He promised to call every Sunday but warned us it would be several months before we would see him again. The car was already packed. Dad cried while he hugged and kissed us good-bye.

Dad kept his promise and called every Sunday. We looked forward to hearing his voice each week. Between phone calls, we were left with memories and objects which reminded us of him.

My brother turned to his toys to fill the emptiness. He would play for hours with fire trucks and airplanes. Our father was a firefighter and enjoyed taking us to the airport to watch planes. These beloved toys were stored safely in Ed's closet. They were his most prized possessions.

One afternoon, shortly after dad moved away, I glanced into my brother's bedroom and saw all of his favorite fire trucks and airplanes thrown throughout the room. A lump instantly formed in my throat. I knew where he was and what he was doing. He was sitting in the dark closet sobbing.

I walked in, shut the door, and gave him a big hug. I asked him what was wrong, and choked up as I felt what he was going through by the broken sound in his little voice. This was the first of many days that we would find comfort together in an empty, dark place.

We would sit in Ed's closet and cry until we felt better—sometimes it took hours. This was our shelter, a place to show the emotions that we didn't know how to control.

Finally, when the world seemed a little brighter, we would bring a small black and white television into the closet and watch our favorite shows together. This spot was small but the feelings were big. It was a place for us to shed tears, share our scars, and heal our hurts.

It's been years, and I still feel those moments like they were yesterday. I can't change the past and wouldn't even if it were possible. When I look back to that period of time, I cherish every moment because something grew big and strong out of that dark closet—my love for my brother Ed.

I believe in the sun even when it is not shining.

I believe in love even when I feel it not.

I believe in God even when He is silent.

WRITTEN ON A WALL IN A CONCENTRATION CAMP

Through a Father's Eyes

LONNI COLLINS PRATT

I saw the car just before it hit me. I seemed to float. Then darkness smashed my senses.

I came to in an ambulance. Opening my eyes, I could see only shreds of light through my bandaged, swollen eyelids. I didn't know it then, but small particles of gravel and dirt were embedded in my freckled sixteen-year-old face. As I tried to touch it, someone tenderly pressed my arm down and whispered. "Lie still."

A wailing siren trailed distantly somewhere, and I slipped into unconsciousness. My last thoughts were a desperate prayer: "Dear God, not my face, please…"

Like many teenage girls, I found much of my identity in my appearance. Adolescence revolved around my outside image. Being pretty meant I had lots of dates and a wide circle of friends.

My father doted on me. He had four sons, but only one daughter. I remember one Sunday in particular. As we got out of the car at church, my brothers—a scruffy threesome in corduroy and cowlicks—ran ahead. Mom had stayed home with the sick baby.

I was gathering my small purse, church school papers, and Bible. Dad opened the door. I looked up at him, convinced in my seven-year-old heart that he was more handsome and smelled better than any daddy anywhere.

He extended his hand to me with a twinkle in his eye and said, "A hand, my lady?" Then he swept me up into his arms and told me how pretty I was. "No father has ever loved a little girl more than I love you," he said.

In my child's heart, which didn't really understand a father's love, I thought it was my pretty dress and face he loved.

A few weeks before the accident, I had won first place in a local pageant, making me the festival queen. Dad didn't say much. He just stood beside me with his arm over my shoulders, beaming with pride. Once more I was his pretty little girl, and I basked in the warmth of his love and acceptance.

About this time, I made a personal commitment to Christ. In the midst of student council, honor society, pageants and parades, I was beginning a relationship with God.

In the hours immediately after my accident, I drifted in and out of consciousness and whenever my mind cleared even slightly, I wondered about my face. I was bleeding internally and had a severe concussion, but it never occurred to me that my concern with appearance was dispropor-tionate.

The next morning, although I couldn't open my eyes more than a slit, I asked the nurse for a mirror. "You just concern yourself with getting well, young lady," she said, not looking at my face as she took my blood pressure.

Her refusal to give me a mirror only fueled irrational determination. If she wouldn't give me a mirror, I reasoned, it must be worse than I imag-ined. My face felt tight and itchy. It burned sometimes and ached other times. I didn't touch it, though, because my doctor told me that might cause infection.

My parents also battled to keep mirrors away. As my strength returned, I became increasingly difficult.

At one point, for the fourth time in less than an hour, I pleaded for a mirror. Five days had passed since the accident.

Angry and beaten down, Dad snapped, "Don't ask again! I said no and that's it!"

I wish I could offer an excuse for what I said. I propped myself on my elbows, and through lips that could barely move, hissed, "You don't love me. Now that I'm not pretty anymore, you just don't love me!"

Dad looked as if someone had knocked the life out of him. He slumped into a chair and put his head in his hands. My mother walked over and put her hand on his shoulder as he tried to control his tears. I collapsed against the pillows.

I didn't ask my parents for a mirror again. Instead, I waited until someone from housekeeping was straightening my room the next morning.

My curtain was drawn as if I were taking a sponge bath. "Could you get me a mirror, please?" I asked. "I must have mislaid mine." After a little searching, she found one and discreetly handed it to me around the curtain.

Nothing could have prepared me for what I saw. An image that resembled a giant scraped knee, oozing and bright pink, looked out at me. My eyes and lips were crusted and swollen. Hardly a patch of skin, ear to ear, had escaped the trauma.

My father arrived a little later with magazines and homework tucked under his arm. He found me staring into the mirror. Prying my fingers one by one from the mirror, he said, "It isn't important. This doesn't change anything that matters. No one will love you less."

Finally he pulled the mirror away and tossed it into a chair. He sat on the edge of my bed, took me in his arms, and held me for a long time.

"I know what you think," he said.

"You couldn't," I mumbled, turning away and staring out the window.

"You're wrong," he said, ignoring my self-pity.

"This will not change anything," he repeated. He put his hand on my arm, running it over an IV line. "The people who love you have seen you at your worst, you know."

"Right, seen me with rollers or with cold cream—not with my face ripped off!"

"Let's talk about me then," he said. "I love you. Nothing will ever change that because it's you I love, not your outside. I've changed your diapers and watched your skin blister with chicken pox. I've wiped up your bloody noses and held your head while you threw up in the toilet. I've loved you when you weren't pretty."

He hesitated. "Yesterday you were ugly—not because of your skin, but because you behaved ugly. But I'm here today, and I'll be here tomorrow. Fathers don't stop loving their children, no matter what life takes. You will be blessed if life only takes your face."

I turned to my father, feeling it was all words, the right words, spoken out of duty—polite lies.

"Look at me then, Daddy," I said. "Look at me and tell me you love me."

I will never forget what happened next. As he looked into my battered face, his eyes filled with tears. Slowly, he leaned toward me, and with his eyes open, he gently kissed my scabbed, oozing lips.

It was the kiss that tucked me in every night of my young life, the kiss that warmed each morning.

Many years have passed. All that remains of my accident is a tiny indentation just above one eyebrow. But my father's kiss, and what it taught me about love, will never leave my lips.

A Letter to My Friends

SARAH REHNBERG
AGE 15

magine:
You are a high schooler who has just survived your third day of school. As you drive home in your mom's stuffy, smelly, purple minivan, you reflect on the day—math (homework) then English (homework), and after lunch economics (homework), and lastly history (homework). Your mom gets off the cell phone, relays some relatively bad news, and then speaks the news that makes your heart soar…you get to stop at 7-Eleven on the way home! Finally your day is looking up! A slurpee. That is all your mind can think of. As you slowly lift the straw up to your lips, you know that with every sip of the life-renewing potion your worries will seem to disappear. Suddenly like a bomb going off in your head, it hits you—you have no control over your lower lip. Therefore, you are not capable to pull them together tight enough around the straw to pull the drink into your mouth. Refusing to give up, you take your fingers and press your lips around the straw and suck. The cool, half-frozen liquid seeps into your mouth, melting onto your tongue. But it seems that is all. The renewing sensation you had been dreaming about was not there and seems to have been forgotten. The sinking fear, that same fear you have experienced so many times these last few days, enters your heart as you realize your whole mouth is numb.

Welcome to my world. Bell's Palsy. It is a virus, as is the common cold, that somehow got into my nervous system and irritated the nerve on the right side of my face. The area that is affected spans from the top of my right eye to the bottom of my chin. This entire area has gone completely numb. When I blink, the right eye does not close all the way. When I talk my lower lip does not move. If I laugh (which occurs often) my left eye squints and lips go up, but nothing happens to the right half of my face. I look like I am mutating or have had a stroke. So sorry to disappoint you, but it is just a virus.

Now I hope you all are wondering why I am writing this to you, because I am about to tell you. It all started on Monday. See, I had this horrible shooting pain up the back of my neck. Then in my head, on the right side, was a small pain. Come Tuesday it was almost unbearable. So, come Wednesday, I was at the doctor's office, being told I had pulled a muscle, which aggravated the nerve to result in the numbness. I was then handed muscle relaxers and a hot pad to help with the pain. By Thursday I had my mom call the doctor, who told us about the virus. When I heard that, I thought there is no way I am going to reexplain my hunchback appearance…thus this letter was written.

In summary, I am now on steroids (of all drugs) and have been, *for the time being,* removed from the volleyball court. It should only take a couple of weeks to clear up. Being restricted from volleyball hurts more than if my entire face were to be paralyzed for life.

In any bad time, as humans we gripe and complain. I refuse to follow this pattern that has so shrewdly been planted by our society. I have learned just how perfect our Creator's timing truly is, and know I am in His all-knowing hands. Thus, I choose to profit from this. I am going to gain a powerful weapon—empathy. Empathy for all the disfigured people in the world. Empathy for anyone who has had a stroke. Empathy for the friendless child who's drooling in class, allowed much snickering and mocking from his classmates. The only difference is that God did not will I suffer for long. I fiercely believe I will be better equipped for ministry because of this. I have also learned how empty and discouraging pity is. I do not ask for pity—it is vain and unnecessary. God has handpicked me to bestow this blessing upon, and I believe when God bestows a blessing, the entire world changes. I do ask for encouragement and prayer—two assets of life. I therefore believe you too can grow from this because you have a choice to make: mock or love. Free will is a funny thing....

Our greatest glory consists not in never falling, but in rising every time we fall.

RALPH WALDO EMERSON

My Favorite Father's Day

JERRY HARPT

With the exception of senior league baseball, my son, Kotter, spent most of the summer after his freshman year of high school home alone. He wasn't happy.

Without any malice on Kotter's part, he made a typical adolescent mistake that caused the loss of his closest friends. He would call them on the phone, but they were too busy to talk. He would bike over to their houses, but they were always gone. He often walked with his head down or stared out the window at nothing. I watched the hurt overflow in Kotter and bled for him as well.

I decided to give up what I too often considered my own precious activities and help Kotter through this stormy, confusing period in his life. When Kotter was younger he often called me his best friend. Now I would work to earn that privileged title.

So I became Kotter's buddy during the summer ball season. I biked with him to and from games. I took him camping. We went to movies. I cheered Kotter's accomplishments and comforted him in his failures. In short, I had become the best friend that he saw me as.

Little by little, as the senior league season moved deeper into summer, I saw signs that the ice curtain of lost friendship was starting to melt. First, it was his teammates' handclasps after a good play. Then it was the shouts of encouragement from the dugout. I pointed these signs out to

Kotter and encouraged him to hang in there. Kotter and I, each in our own way, used these proclamations as our banners of hope.

During the latter part of June, a senior league tournament was held in Marinette, Wisconsin. It was held on Father's Day weekend, and Kotter's team earned the right to play in the championship game, which was held on Father's Day. The evenly matched teams took turns taking the lead. Near the end of the game, Kotter's team was behind by one run, had a man on base, and Kotter was up to bat. He walked up to the batter's box as tension filled the air. He would not be denied encouragement from his friends at that moment. "You can do it, Kotter," and "Come on, big boy," rang out from the dugout. Kotter fed on this affection as he stepped into the batter's box. I cheered from the stands as well. I cheered for Kotter, and I cheered inside for the affection I saw coming from the dugout.

CRACK! The soft spot of the bat connected perfectly with the ball and sent it screaming out into left field! This ball was tagged! I gripped the edge of my seat and held my breath in disbelief. The left fielder stopped running, turned around, and watched the ball sail over the fence. The home run sealed the victory for Kotter's team.

Pandemonium broke out in the crowd of spectators. Every person was standing up and celebrating except for one. I remained seated, trying to control my emotions and thanking God for answered prayers. The homerun, no doubt, made me happy, but the scene at home plate over-whelmed me. My son, whose heart bled so profusely these past months, was now being hugged by his teammates as they marched triumphantly to the dugout.

Once I composed myself, I hurried to the fence near the dugout to celebrate Kotter's homerun and to celebrate something even deeper—to celebrate the resurrection of human spirit that was occurring within him.

When I reached the fence I saw something else that tugged at my emotions. I saw an old friend and teammate hand Kotter the homerun ball that the friend had retrieved from outside the park. The gesture brought back memories of the same two boys riding their bikes together the previous summer. I turned from the crowd so my lips could quiver more freely.

After the victory celebration, I went for a long walk to reflect on the game. I thought about the home run that fulfilled, for my son, a dream that all kids have. I thought about the crisis that helped strengthen the relationship I had with him. Most of all, I thought about the human spirit's ability to revive itself after letdown. This was truly the best Father's Day I could ever imagine.

Yet, the warmest moment was still to come. When I got home that day, I spotted a baseball, with writing on it, sitting on the kitchen table. I picked up the ball, read the inscription, and started to cry. The ball I held was my son's home run ball, and the inscription read: "Happy Father's Day, Dad! Love, Kotter."

Courage is fear that's said its prayers.

AUTHOR UNKNOWN

Eagle's Wings

But those who hope in the LORD will renew their strength.
They will soar on wings like eagles.

ISAIAH 40:31

Seeing Beyond

MORT CRIM
FROM *THE JOY OF GOOD NEWS*

Erik was barely fourteen when he joined his high school wrestling team in Phoenix. Soon, he was named co-captain. And not long after that, he became state champion runner-up in his class. Erik was born to be competitive. Mostly he competed with himself, taking on personal challenges, such as rock climbing. In 1995 he scaled Mt. McKinley—at twenty-thousand feet, the highest peak in North America. Then he took on the three-thousand-foot granite monolith, El Capitan, in Yosemite.

Erik wasn't the first person ever to scale El Capitan. But he was the first blind person to do it. Erik was born with a rare, degenerative eye disease and was completely blind by age thirteen, sightless before he accomplished any of these feats. But Erik will tell you blindness isn't a disability. It's only a nuisance. It doesn't mean you can't do things. It just means you have to find different ways of doing them.

A disability is in the body.

A handicap is in the mind.

Too many of us make the mistake of not distinguishing one from the other.

Enjoy the Ride!

BARBARA JOHNSON
FROM *JOY BREAKS*

Yesterday is a sacred room in your heart where you keep your memories. Here you cherish laughter from another day. You hear melodies of half-forgotten songs. You feel the warmth of a hug from an old friend. You see the lingering glow of a long-gone love. From your yesterdays you draw lessons and encouragement to pass along to others.

My heart smiled at some yesterdays recently when I thought back on teaching my oldest son, Tim, how to drive. We practiced in a nearby cemetery where it was quiet, the posted speed limits were very slow, and traffic was sparse. *A nice, safe place to start,* I thought.

Tim would work his way around the curves and turns, carefully maneuvering the car through its paces. Brake into the curve. Gently. Accelerate out of the curve. Slowly. Smoothly. Stop. Reverse. Back up. Park between the lines. Try it again. Start all over again.

Afterward, we'd go over to In-N-Out Hamburgers across the street where I would recover from the experience. After we ate, Tim would want to tackle the curves again. Sometimes I wondered if I would survive until he actually learned how to drive.

Well, I did. Tim did learn. And he was a good driver. But years later, his car was smashed by someone who wasn't. Now, Tim's grave is right up there where he practiced driving.

I could be bitter about it. Or I can be better. When yesterdays bring bittersweet memories, I can fume and blame my losses on someone else, or I can let my memories comfort me and provide encouragement to someone else.

As I was standing by Tim's grave recently and thinking of the many times we wound around those curving lanes, I remembered how I used to feel: nervous and tense but trying not to show it. My reverie by Tim's headstone was interrupted when a little red Nissan came around the curve. There was a mother, about thirty-five, her hair blowing in the breeze. Beside her, in the driver's seat, sat a boy, about fifteen, cute as anything. The mom's face looked intent while the boy tried to look nonchalant.

I wanted to shout out, "Enjoy the ride! Now! Make a memory of your experience. Go get a hamburger to celebrate. Do it now, while you still can look each other in the eyes!"

Yes, it hurts. I wish Tim were here, driving me to some of the places I need to go occasionally, just for old times' sake. I long for the family circle—unbroken—the way it will be in heaven. I want to hear my boy's laughter again and the way he used to rush in the house and call, "Mom!" I envy that mom in the little red Nissan, but I know the years end up stealing something from everybody. And I just want to tell that woman to savor the moment. Taste the present full strength. Do everything you can to hold it close.

This week when I go do the things I have to do, I'll take my own advice. I'll look people in the eyes, and if they don't have a smile, I'll give them one of mine. I'll make a date with my husband or play a joke on a friend. I won't let time pass without reminding myself, "Enjoy the ride!"

Tragedy to Triumph

FROM *GOD'S LITTLE LESSONS ON LIFE FOR GRADUATES*

One winter night, a man was driving two young women to a meeting when they came upon a multiple-car collision. They were unable to stop on the slick road before they slammed into the back of a car. One of the girls, Donna, was thrown face-first through the windshield. The jagged edges of the broken windshield made horrible gashes in her face.

At the hospital, a plastic surgeon took great care in stitching Donna's face. Nevertheless, the driver dreaded visiting Donna. He expected to find her sad and depressed. Instead, he found her happy and bright, refusing to let the accident destroy her joy.

As Donna slowly recovered she became intrigued by the work of the doctors and nurses. She later studied and became a nurse, met a young doctor, married him, and then had two children. Years later she admitted that the accident was one of the best things that ever happened to her.

A Father's Love

JASON RANDLE
AGE 17

t was a Saturday morning in March; I was fourteen years old. My dad and I were watching the college football game; this had become a custom in our house on Saturday, Sunday, and Monday nights in the fall and winter. Our favorite college team, the Huskies, had just scored their second touchdown, bringing them to fourteen points. My dad and I each got down on our hands and knees and proceeded to do our fourteen push-ups to match their score, our tradition when watching the Huskies play. These were times I cherished most with my dad.

However, all this would come to an abrupt halt the next morning at about seven o'clock when the phone piercingly rang. It brought news of my father being hospitalized. With no idea of the severity of his injury, the car ride to the hospital seemed unending to me. My father's boss met us at the hospital, but refused to tell us what had happened, which only made things worse for my mom, my sister, and me. Walking with my eyes fixed on the hospital door, I could only imagine what shocks and terrifying news were sure to come.

After what seemed an eternity, I finally reached the double doors and pulled them open as fast as I could. I didn't even think to hold them open for anyone else. Finally we reached the elevator that would take us to the floor of my father's broken existence and reveal to us what was to lie ahead. Convinced the elevator was not going fast enough, I screamed out, "Come on!" in hopes of speeding it up, which did not seem to work. But eventually I heard the ding that was followed by the opening of the elevator doors. I stepped out into what could quite possibly turn into my own personal hell. Arlon, my dad's boss, led us to where we could wait for news of my father's condition, news that would change the course of our whole life.

Walking down the halls toward our waiting room, I saw a woman with her hand over her face, crying, being led by a doctor. I wondered if that would soon be me. But I tried my best to keep some form of hope. My dad permanently leaving my family was not an option I was willing to even consider. We finally reached the room where we could sit and wait for some form of professional update of how my father was doing. We were finally told by my dad's boss what had happened. While at work he was run over by a front end loader. My mind raced after that, going back and forth, wondering how he could have survived even this long. Sitting on the surprisingly comfortable couches, I found myself looking at all the paintings on the wall. At a time like this, flowers and pink were the last things I wanted to look at. Being at such an awful place emotionally, even pretty colors and pictures could not make me smile. Nothing could, except the one thing out of my reach, my dad's well-being. Just as I looked out the open door into the hallway, I saw doctors running while pushing a bed. As I looked up, I noticed the man on the bed. *This lifeless figure of a man was my father.*

Immediately following him was a doctor who came in and told us to follow him to intensive care where they were taking my dad. We followed the doctor into the elevator. I hoped he would say something, but no words came out of his mouth. We reached the somewhat bigger room where friends and some family had shown up, but no one was able to help me. It seemed as though not a person on this earth could get a smile out of me; with the hand I had been dealt I had no reason to smile.

I heard a noise somewhere around and looked to find the door handle turning and saw the door slowly opening. A foot with a white shoe was set in front of us; then the other white shoe was placed beside it. I looked up to see the downcast face of a doctor. Though he said a lot, all I heard was murmuring, a muffled voice going into my ear. The only words I was able to hear were the worst I had ever heard: "Survival is not guaranteed." Those few words hit me up the side of the head and on my chest with the same power and overwhelming strength as a bowling ball flying through pins without effort. This was the most awful experience I had ever had to endure. Then came the tears. I cried until my whole body became numb, and in the midst of all this, I felt an arm, a strong, loving arm, embrace me. I lifted my eyes up to see whom the arm belonged to, but there was no one. I realized then that it was the gentle, loving arm of God.

Saturday I returned to the hospital and was told that I should say good-bye to my dad in case he would not live through the next night. So I was led to the room where he was, broken and battered, and I looked deep into his eyes as he looked into mine. He was unable to speak, though he tried to anyway. He was rudely interrupted by the tube which was preventing him from telling me what I already knew: the fact that, no matter what, he loved me.

The next day I lost my best friend in the world. This whole ordeal was a nightmare, one from which I expected to wake up, but I haven't yet. Yet despite everything I've gone through, and the pain I've seen, I know I've come to realize that God is telling the truth when He says, "I'll be a Father to the fatherless." And I understand how God is our source of all comfort. Like what Scripture says in 2 Corinthians 1:4, God comforts us in all our troubles. I now find that to be true.

I have lost my earthly father, but I have gained a heavenly Father. I may have lost everything, but I've also gained everything.

Welcoming Amy

NANCY JO SULLIVAN
FROM *MOMENTS OF GRACE*

i t had been fifteen years since her abortion, but every Mother's Day, Marie still found herself conversing with a child she had never held.

"What do you look like? Do you sing in heaven? I sure love you," she whispered.

Now thirty-five, Marie had directed the Crisis Pregnancy Center's ministry for five years. She worked there today, even though it was Sunday and Mother's Day. Small silver-framed photos decorated her office: pictures of young mothers and newborn infants, all giving gentle testimony to life, freely chosen.

She remembered the unborn baby she had carried in her womb for two and a half months.

When Marie was nineteen years old, she was unmarried and pregnant. Embarrassed and ashamed of her secret, Marie had decided not to seek help from her family. "It would disgrace us," she thought. She scheduled an abortion.

However, for the next five years, her decision brought her unending depression and remorse.

Only by grace had Marie found healing at a church that welcomed her, supporting her through weeks of postabortion counseling. At this church she had met countless women like her, who, in a vulnerable moment, had chosen abortion.

With their help, she had learned to balance the horrors of terminating a pregnancy with the relentless forgiveness of God.

"I'll never stop helping others to choose life," Marie promised her baby.

She fingered a silver-framed photo on her desk. The phone rang.

"Happy Mother's Day," Marie greeted the caller. On the other end of the line a woman was crying.

"I need some help," she said.

"I can give that," Marie assured her.

Homeless and four months pregnant, a nineteen-year-old named Amy was calling from a pay phone. The father of her child was a chronic abuser; now he had left her to deal with the pregnancy alone.

"I don't want an abortion, but I don't have another choice," she said.

Marie reached into her purse and pulled out a cross necklace. Though it was ornate and much too large to wear, Marie always carried it with her. During her postabortion counseling, it had been given to her by an elderly woman named Hilda.

Though Hilda had a secret abortion in the 1950s, she had shamelessly offered Marie an invitation to receive the love of God. It was Hilda who had welcomed Marie into the family of faith.

"You do have another choice," Marie told the caller as she clutched the cross. "I'll help you," Marie added.

Continuing to comfort the pregnant woman, Marie gave her reassurances about temporary shelter and medical care.

"Do you have a family?" Marie asked. Amy had grown up in an abusive home; it was unsafe for her to seek refuge there.

"I have grandparents...but I haven't seen them since I was two years old," Amy said. "I don't think they would remember me."

Later that evening, while Amy found rest and comfort in a transitional home supervised by center volunteers, Marie called Amy's grandparents in Hawaii.

"Hello, my name is Marie. I direct a Crisis Pregnancy Center in Minnesota," Marie told Amy's relatives.

As Marie told Amy's plight, the elderly couple listened carefully and asked questions. Their first concern was for their granddaughter's welfare.

"Is she okay? Is the boyfriend still abusing her? When is the baby due?" they asked.

After a few moments of reflection, Amy's grandparents agreed to take her in. "God is calling us to help her," they told Marie.

Over the next few days, Marie worked out the arrangements for Amy to join her grandparents. She secured a plane ticket to Hawaii from the board of directors at the center. Other ministry volunteers filled a secondhand suitcase with brand new maternity clothes and a layette for the baby. Still another volunteer dropped off a check for twenty-five dollars.

"Give this to Amy," he instructed. "Tell her she can spend it any way she likes."

The day of Amy's departure arrived. At the airport, Marie and Amy waited on the concourse for a plane that would take Amy to her waiting grandparents.

"You've given me the courage to bring my baby into the world," Amy told Marie. "I want to raise my child right."

"God will help you," Marie said.

"God?" Amy's face looked puzzled.

"Yes. God loves you very much," Marie said.

"Me? He loves me?" This was the first time anyone had said this to her.

In the next few minutes, as harried passengers scurried by with luggage, the two women talked of God's power, His forgiveness, His plan for Amy and her baby.

"God is waiting to welcome you into His family," Marie said softly.

Amy nodded. For her, it was a moment of quiet conversion.

As the two women clasped hands to pray, Marie felt the inner nudging of God.

"Why don't you give Amy the cross necklace?" a voice in her heart suggested.

No, Marie thought. Not the necklace.

But as the airport intercom summoned the passengers to a plane bound for Hawaii, Marie reached into her purse and placed the cross in Amy's hand.

Amy's face beamed. Marie watched as the young teenage mother put the necklace on over her brand new maternity top.

"This will be the first thing my baby wears," she said as she gave Marie one last hug.

As Amy made her way toward the plane, Marie prayed that Hilda's cross would sustain the young mother through all the uncertain days ahead; that it would always remind Amy that she was now a loved member of God's family.

"Family," Marie whispered as she wondered how Amy would recognize the grandparents she hadn't seen in years.

Just before Amy disappeared down the concourse, Marie called out to her: "How will you know your grandparents?"

Amy turned around, one of her hands clutching the cross hanging around her neck. Her face was full of joy as she called back: "They told me to look for a WELCOME, AMY sign!"

I'm carrying the world today,
it's too big for me.
So dear Lord, I was wondering if
you could carry me?

AUTHOR UNKNOWN

it's a God Thing

God, remember the time we played together;
you were a rainbow and I slid down your colors.
I danced beneath your brilliant light,
and that night you covered me with your colors,
and I was safe.

KRISTINE MINIONE
PRESENTATION HIGH SCHOOL
FROM *DREAMS ALIVE*

My First Christmas in Heaven

AUTHOR UNKNOWN

This poem is alleged to have been written by a teen boy who died of a brain tumor he had battled for four years. He gave this to his mom before he died.

I see the countless Christmas trees
Around the world below
With tiny lights, like heaven's stars,
Reflecting on the snow.

The sight is so spectacular,
Please wipe away the tear
For I am spending Christmas with
Jesus Christ this year.

I hear the many Christmas songs,
That people hold so dear
But the sounds of music can't compare
With the Christmas choir up here.

I have no words to tell you,
The joy their voices bring,

For it is beyond description,
To hear the angels sing.

I know how much you miss me,
I see the pain inside your heart.
But I am not so far away,
We really aren't apart.

So be happy for me, dear ones,
You know I hold you dear.
And be glad I'm spending Christmas
With Jesus Christ this year.

I sent you each a special gift,
From my heavenly home above.
I sent you each a memory
Of my undying love.

After all, love is a gift more precious
Than pure gold.
It was always most important
In the stories Jesus told.

Please love and keep each other,
As my Father said to do.
For I can't count the blessings of love
He has for each of you.

So have a Merry Christmas and
Wipe away that tear.
Remember, I am spending Christmas with
Jesus Christ this year.

Daddy's Day

CHERYL L. COSTELLO-FORSHEY
FROM *HEARTPRINTS*

Her hair up in a ponytail, her favorite dress tied with a bow
Today was Daddy's Day at school, and she couldn't wait to go
But her mommy tried to tell her, that she probably should stay home
Why the kids might not understand, if she went to school alone
But she was not afraid; she knew just what to say
What to tell her classmates, on this Daddy's Day
But still her mother worried, for her to face this day alone
And that was why once again, she tried to keep her daughter home
But the little girl went to school, eager to tell them all
About a dad she never sees, a dad who never calls.

There were daddies along the wall in back, for everyone to meet
Children squirming impatiently, anxious in their seats
One by one the teacher called, a student from the class
To introduce their daddy, as seconds slowly passed
At last the teacher called her name, every child turned to stare
Each of them was searching, for a man that wasn't there
"Where's her daddy at?" She heard a boy call out
"She probably doesn't have one." Another student dared to shout
And from somewhere near the back, she heard a daddy say
"Looks like another deadbeat dad, too busy to waste his day."
The words did not offend her, as she smiled at her friends

And looked back at her teacher, who told her to begin
And with hands behind her back, slowly she began to speak
And out from the mouth of a child, came words incredibly unique
"My daddy couldn't be here, because he lives so far away
But I know he wishes he could be with me on this day
And though you cannot meet him, I wanted you to know
All about my daddy, and how much he loves me so
He loved to tell me stories, he taught me to ride my bike
He surprised me with pink roses, and he taught me to fly a kite
We used to share fudge sundaes, and ice cream in a cone
And though you cannot see him, I'm not standing all alone
'Cause my daddy's always with me, even though we are apart
I know because he told me, he'll forever be here in my heart."

With that her little hand reached up, and lay across her chest
Feeling her own heartbeat, beneath her favorite dress
And from somewhere in the crowd of dads, her mother stood in tears
Proudly watching her daughter, who was wise beyond her years
For she stood up for the love of a man not in her life
Doing what was best for her, doing what was right
And when she dropped her hand back down, staring straight into the crowd
She finished with a voice so soft, but its message clear and loud.

"I love my daddy very much, he's my shining star
And if he could he'd be here, but heaven's just too far
But sometimes when I close my eyes, it's like he never went away."
And then she closed her eyes, and saw him there that day
And to her mother's amazement, she witnessed with surprise
A room full of daddies and children, all starting to close their eyes
Who knows what they saw before them, who knows what they felt inside
Perhaps for merely a second, they saw him at her side.
"I know you're with me, Daddy." To the silence she called out

And what happened next made believers of those once filled with doubt
Not one in that room could explain it, for each of their eyes had been closed
But there placed on her desktop was a beautiful fragrant pink rose
And a child was blessed, if only a moment, by the love of her shining bright star
And given the gift of believing that heaven is never too far.

The Lord your God is with you,
he is mighty to save.
He will take great delight in you,
he will quiet you with his love,
he will rejoice over you with singing.

ZEPHANIAH 3:17
FROM *THE HOLY BIBLE*

Crazy About You

If God had a refrigerator, your picture would be on it.
If He had a wallet, your photo would be in it.
He sends you flowers every spring and a sunrise every morning.
Whenever you want to talk, He'll listen.
He can live anywhere in the universe, but He chose your heart.
What about the Christmas gift He sent you in Bethlehem,
not to mention that Friday at Calvary.
Face it, He's crazy about you.

MAX LUCADO
FROM *A GENTLE THUNDER*

A Sure Sign

=◎=

YITTA HALBERSTAM AND JUDITH LEVENTHAL
FROM *SMALL MIRACLES*

Linda Valentine was a famous model. Yet despite her money, fame, and glamour she felt a gnawing emptiness inside. There was a sense of unease she could not cast off, a restlessness of spirit that filled her with unspeakable anxiety and dread. At night, she was plagued with insomnia. She began to ask her friends what they thought of taking prescription drugs like Xanax and Valium.

While many of them obligingly described the relative merits of each, one friend looked at Linda with genuine concern and took her aside. "That's not what you need," she whispered in distress. "Popping pills will only do you harm. And they only mask the symptoms, they don't address them. Are you free this weekend?"

That weekend Linda's friend took her to a program called Impact that promised to help participants articulate and accomplish their goals. It delivered.

Incredibly, within a short week of taking the seminar, Linda achieved career breakthroughs and won contracts she had been dreaming about for years. But despite the sudden fulfillment of her greatest ambitions, her general insecurity lingered. Her soul remained in torment.

One morning she was taking her usual route to work, driving down

La Brea, the main thoroughfare, when traffic came to a standstill. A water main had broken, and traffic was being diverted to a small, obscure street, one that she had never driven down before. As she inched her car along the unfamiliar street, she noticed a small storefront church with a handwritten sign in its window that proclaimed: "No God, no peace. Know God, know peace. Everybody welcome." *Hmm,* she thought as she drove slowly by, *how quaint!*

The next morning Linda was on her way to work again, driving down La Brea, when, for the second day in a row, traffic came to a halt. A fire was blazing out of control in one of the shops lining the boulevard, and fire trucks were converging on the scene from all directions. Policemen blocked off the area and diverted traffic to the same obscure street as the day before. "Oh, no!" she groaned, "not again!" Once again she drove by the small storefront church. This time the sign seemed compelling, not quaint. She thought for a moment that it was summoning her inside. "What an imagination I have!" she laughed, scolding herself for her penchant for melodrama. Still, from her car window, she squinted at the storefront church, trying to catch a glimpse of its interior. Her gaze was wistful.

The next day she thought of changing routes, but told herself that she was being foolish. After all, what were the odds of another calamity occurring on the same street three days in a row? "This will be a test," she chuckled to herself. "If there's some disaster on La Brea again, and traffic gets diverted down that same street again, then I'll know for sure it's a sign!"

When she turned down La Brea, she was thunderstruck. Traffic was backed up for blocks. A major car accident, explained an apologetic cop, diverting traffic again, for the third time in a row, down the same small street. "That does it!" she exclaimed. She parked her car and entered the church, which was empty except for a young priest sitting behind a desk. He looked up at her and smiled. "What took you so long?" he asked.

He had seen her car pass by all three days and had absorbed her wistful gaze. They spoke for a long time, and she joined the congregation. That was eighteen years ago, and she's been there ever since, having found the peace and serenity that had eluded her elsewhere. Just as the sign promised, what she had really needed in her life was God. And wasn't it, after all, God who had sent her there in the first place?

God does not love us because we are valuable.
We are valuable because God loves us.

ARCHBISHOP FULTON J. SHEEN

My Life in a Box

DON OTT

Mark, the youth pastor, calls, wanting help with another of his creative messages to teens. "You're just the man for the job," he gushes. "You're perfect for playing a dead guy."

While I ponder that compliment, he explains that the next youth group meeting falls on October 31, Halloween. Ghosts. Goblins. Dead guys. He plans to illustrate the fragility of life by recreating a funeral complete with candles, crying sister, childhood friend, eulogy, coffin, and dead guy. "They'll believe it's real," he chuckles.

Even though I know better, a "Yes" escapes my lips.

The commitment sealed, Mark reveals that the "deceased" will actually be in "the box," a real coffin loaned by a mortuary. I freeze. *In* a coffin? Feebly I manage to ask, "It isn't used, is it?" New, he promises. "Open or closed?" Open, he assures me.

I'm in. Literally.

Now, spending a workday knowing that your funeral is set for the close of business tends to make you professionally unproductive. I fidget and squirm, preparing to climb into the coffin, a real one off the showroom floor. "It's an act," I murmur. But that waiting coffin strikes a chord deep inside, requiring me to acknowledge my mortality.

Mark's next call interrupts a nerve-racking Halloween afternoon, and my hopes rise. A cancellation?

"All set!" he chirps.

"Great," I intone. "Rats," I mean.

That evening, my widow-to-be offers me my last meal of leftover fast food chicken with fresh mashed potatoes. About to be dead, I see no reason to eat the cauliflower. For obvious reasons, I avoid fluids. I pop an antihistamine lest my growing casket allergy result in undead-guy-like sneezing or coughin'. Dressed in a dark suit, I trudge to my funeral.

The co-conspirators are waiting at the church. "He looks so natural," they joke upon my arrival. I courtesy-laugh and cast a furtive glance down the aisle where the object of my daylong discomfort lurks. The box yawns, waiting, its peach-colored lining highlighting its dark walnut stain. My thoughts turn to a more pleasant walk down an aisle, a beautiful woman in white on my arm. This isn't as appealing.

Pallor-white makeup is rubbed on my face, accompanied by a scolding for not shaving. "I wasn't thinking," I apologize. "I was mostly dead all day."

A woman said that it would require a pill to get her in the box. I need *several* pills. *It's pretend, nothing to it,* I lie to myself. Aware of my pounding heart, I suddenly realize: Pounding is good! Keep pounding!

The sound engineer, a bodybuilder, grabs me and lays me in the coffin like a sleeping child. They arrange the covers, lower the crank a smidgen, and say that everything is perfect. For them. They aren't in the box.

The satin pillow is soft; the other parts aren't. Despite its wooden facade, the box is chilly aluminum with hidden body-support cables running its length. One traverses the middle of my goose-pimpled back, prodding my tailbone. A professional dead guy wouldn't care, I think, grateful for amateur status. My eyes close. Breathe in, breathe out, one hour in the box.

People are talking, but not to me. I'm dead. Someone stage-whispers, "They're coming." Reflections from candles flicker through my closed lids. I wish the organ would play "Great Is Thy Faithfulness," and I make a mental note to write that down, so on my day, it will.

When the young people gather up the hill from the church, Mark explains that they will be attending a funeral for thirty-five-year-old Samuel McNabb. The next-of-kin, from Massachusetts, want their dearly departed memorialized before flying the remains back east for burial. The church has offered to provide some mourners. The solemn teens carry candles and follow an antique hearse. Two hundred attend Samuel's funeral.

My funeral.

Contemplation joins me in that coffin. I pray for my daughters, for the day they'll do this for real, hoping the truth that my soul isn't in the box will give them a measure of comfort. I pray for my wife, who is discharging my annual duty of shepherding trick-or-treaters. "Daddy's dead tonight, girls."

An urgent petition surges for my dad, who, fighting Alzheimer's at eighty-one, may be the next person I see in this position. That sobering thought clangs against the confines of the coffin. Unsure of his relationship to God, I vow to talk to him. Soon.

I pray for the upcoming message and that someone will recognize his need for Jesus. Aware that activities, church and secular, clog my calendar, I pray for a more strategic life. I realize that life's busyness distracts me from recognizing that each sunrise brings my final sunset one day closer.

Footsteps sound quietly from the back of the church as the cortege arrives amid "shushes." The teens shuffle in, unsure if this is for real or not. Some think, *That guy in the box must be fake. But...he sure looks...*dead. I sense their discomfort. *Welcome to the club,* I think, as the cable gouges deeper into my rear.

Eulogizing, my real life long-lost friend recalls how we played baseball. "We'd lost touch lately," he admits, striking close to home. My fake sister, whom I met that night, accurately reveals that I was the baby of the family. She wonders aloud, with theatrical sobs, why God allows a good man to be taken in the prime of life, while rotten people get to live.

Mark then tells the story of Lazarus from John 11. He explains that Jesus knew Lazarus was dying but delayed coming. Arriving days later, He had the stone of the tomb rolled away and called forth Lazarus. Resurrection! Jesus has power over death!

"Some of you are dead spiritually," Mark says. "Today is your day to roll away the stone, to let Jesus give you life." And a girl, appropriately dressed like a butterfly (it is Halloween), realizes it is her day. A new life arises on a day of death. Jesus still gives life.

The guy in the box stiffens as tears squeeze through his clenched eyes.

Mark finishes by asking, "What was it like when Jesus called Lazarus out of the tomb? Wouldn't it be amazing to see that?" He pauses for effect: "Samuel."

Sorry, Samuel's dead.

"Samuel!"

Rigor mortis. Can't move.

"Samuel!!"

"WHAT?!" I roar, bolting upright, raising my hands in exasperation.

Someone screams. Then laughter erupts as the trick becomes a treat. Officially alive again, still in the box, I wave in time to upbeat music. Finally they lift me out and Samuel takes his final bow.

At home, a hot shower melts off the makeup and eases away the remaining tension of the preceding days. As I crawl into bed and thank God for such a landmark day, I realize that I have been impacted as much as anyone in the building.

My life in a box, all sixty minutes of it, continues to remind me of the importance of each moment and to really live while I'm alive.

That...and to screen my calls from Mark more carefully.

The List

JODI DETRICK

Hey, girl! While you were at school today, I was returning something to your room (no, this isn't a lecture about putting things away!) when I spotted a little piece of paper face up on your dresser. I could see at a glance that it was a list of things to do. I'm glad you've picked up my habit of list-making. It sure helps to keep a person on track. And what a sense of accomplishment comes from checking off the final item!

As I got closer to the list, curiosity got the better of me...okay, so I was *slightly* nosy. (It comes with the mom territory!) Anyway, I wondered what you wanted to remember in your busy life today.

You really do have a hectic pace, especially now that you're a senior in high school. I can't remember being quite so busy as you are when I was your age. Besides your daily classes, you've got cheerleading, jazz choir (at 7 A.M. every day!), student council, youth group at church, not to mention talking on the phone and hanging with your friends whenever you can! Then there are scholarships to apply for, colleges to check out, and future plans to think about.

In all that busyness, I wondered what you would write on a "to-do" list. Will you try to remember all that Dad and I have been hoping to build into your life...honesty, compassion, truths from God's Word? Will you remember the other things I've drilled into you like:

buckle up, speak up, cheer up, look up?

You can't blame me for being a little overboard here. After all, you're my *last* child to graduate from high school, and soon you'll be leaving the nest. I think I've caught the syndrome that goes along with such a predicament. It didn't help when you stopped me in the hallway the night before school began and said, "Mom, do you realize this is the last time you'll have a kid starting a new school year in the morning?"

"Thanks a *lot!*" I blubbered as I held you in a Momma-bear hug.

So, I wondered, as I picked up your list, *what's most important for you to remember today? Hmm...* I scan the list.

E-mail Erin.

Fill out senior bio form.

Do worship team schedule.

I continue to read down the list when two words catch my eye. There, right in the middle of your self-reminders like *take $6 to school* and *try on white tee,* I see them and smile.

Love Jesus.

I brush away a tear as I turn off your light and close your door. In the middle of one of the busiest times of your life, you're choosing to remember what Jesus said was the greatest commandment. I wish I could say those two words were always right in the middle of my "to-do" list. Thanks for the reminder of what's really important.

You know what, my last, now-a-senior-and-soon-to-be-leaving-the-nest child? You're going to be just fine. And I think this mother bird is going to make it, too.

Gotta run now, girl! I need to add something to my list.

My Prayer Line

CHRISTINA BOOS
FROM *I'M IN JUNIOR HIGH, BUT IT'S NOT MY FAULT*

I watched as the police car pulled out of my driveway and drove down the street. All I could do now was wait. I walked over to the phone and looked at it, as if my stare could make it ring. I sat next to it and once again reflected on all that had happened.

I remembered walking home from school, just like we always did. Then a car engine rumbled behind us, and as we turned to see what it was, a truck swerved and hit my friend Jamie square in the back. The events that followed happened so fast that it's hard to believe they could have been real—the police, the sirens, the questions from the detective. I could still see them putting Jamie into the ambulance, and I could still hear his screams of pain as they drove away.

R-I-I-I-NG! The piercing ringing of the telephone interrupted my thoughts. I lunged at the phone in hopes that it might be information about Jamie's condition. I pushed the receiver to my ear, my hand shaking all the way.

I had barely uttered a hello, when I heard a computer's voice sing, "This is a survey for a local research company and we'd…" I slammed down the phone and wondered how a device that had given me so much joy could betray me. I thought about all of the times I had talked to Jamie on the phone. I wanted so much for him to call me.

312

My mom walked in the room. "He'll be okay," she said. "God is with him." Then she left.

That one sentence said more to me than any other sentence that I had ever heard in my whole life. At that moment I decided to call God, on my own personal line, through prayer. I asked God to be with Jamie, and I asked Him to hold him in His healing arms. I asked God to be with all of us who care about Jamie, and I asked Him to give us an extra measure of the Holy Spirit so that we could be patient and wait until news of Jamie's condition had a chance to reach us. The minute I said amen the phone rang. The voice on the other end breathed out six words: "He is going to be okay."

Jamie returned to school about a month later, just as happy and healthy as always. To most of those who were affected by the accident, it was history. The case of Jamie's experience may have been closed, but the phone line between me and God would always remain open.

Hope is wishing a thing to come true;
Faith is believing it will come true.

NORMAN VINCENT PEALE

Lost and Found

I was once lost, but now I'm found.
I once wished, but now I dream.
I once received, but now I give.
I once sinned, but now I pray.
I once saw the darkness, but now I see the light.

TIFFANY N. TAYLOR
AGE 17

My Brother's Love

≈◎≈

GARY COBB

In 1972 I was a rebellious teenager. I was involved with alcohol and with drugs. In the autumn of that year my brother, Terry, accepted Jesus Christ. Terry began to tell me about Christ. I thought that Terry was going through a religious phase and that he would be back to normal within a few days. The months went by, and I saw his commitment to the Lord Jesus deepen. Terry continued to pray for me and talk to me about Jesus.

A few days after Christmas Terry was working at a supermarket. As two men left, they grabbed two of the cashiers and at gunpoint the men forced my brother to open the safe. The robbers then took Terry to the back of the store and shot him.

The bullet lodged in Terry's spine; he was paralyzed from the waist down. For two weeks my mother and I stayed day and night at the hospital. God finally had my attention. I thought about what Terry had told me about Jesus.

On New Year's Day 1973, in the hospital prayer room, a number of my mother's Christian friends gathered to pray. That night I prayed, "God, I know I've done many things that are wrong. I'm sorry; please forgive me. I want to give You my life."

I told Terry of my decision to give my life to Christ, saying, "Terry, God has used what has happened to you to speak to me, and I have accepted Christ and I am going to live my life for Him." Terry couldn't speak, but he smiled as he rejoiced in my decision. A few days later he died.

Six months after Terry's death I was working at the same supermarket where Terry had been shot. One day, as I was telling one of the stock boys about Jesus, he said, "Your brother used to tell me the same thing about Christ."

I asked, "What was your reaction to what he said?"

The stock boy replied, "I told him that he ought to talk to you. I told him that his own brother needed Christ more than anyone else I knew."

Interested, I asked, "What did Terry say to that?"

The stock boy replied, "Your brother said that he would give his life if you could come to know the Lord Jesus."

Terry's love and concern for me was exactly what led me to Christ. He loved me so much that he was willing to die so that I could find real life in Christ. Terry's sacrificial love has been a constant reminder of a greater love and sacrifice.

Jesus loves us, and He proved it by dying for us all. My greatest joy is to tell others of His love for them.

This article was taken from Decision *magazine, Oct. 2000, ©2000 Billy Graham Evangelistic Association. Used by permission, all rights reserved.*

*All I have seen teaches me
to trust the Creator for all I have not seen.*

RALPH WALDO EMERSON

The Man from Sydney

RETOLD BY ALICE GRAY

On that rainy night in Liverpool, England, the tent was packed. One woman stood out among the more than seven hundred people who came to worship that first night. Her face seemed to shine as she sang. When the music ended, the preacher singled her out: "Sister, do you have a word for the Lord?"

Without hesitating, she stood. "I do," she called out, her face alive with joy. "Eight years ago, as I walked down George Street in Sydney, Australia, an old man in ragged clothes stopped me. 'Excuse me, ma'am,' he said. 'if you were to die tonight, where would you spend eternity?'

"His question kept coming back into my thoughts. Finally, I talked to the pastor of a church near my home. Then I started reading the Bible and found out what it meant to become a Christian. One day, I asked Jesus to forgive my sins and to come into my life as Lord and Savior.

"Since then I have never doubted that when I die, I will spend eternity in heaven with Him."

On the second night of the weeklong crusade, the crowd overflowed. As the preacher searched the sea of new faces, his eyes were drawn to a young man. "Brother," he asked, "do you have a testimony for the Lord?"

The young man leaped to his feet. "When I was stationed in Sydney, Australia, during my military service a few years ago, an old man in ragged clothes came up to me and asked if I knew where I'd spend eternity if I died that same night.

"Well, I couldn't go to sleep that night. I thought about the things my Christian parents had taught me, the stories I learned in Sunday school. Very early the next morning I knelt beside my bunk and asked Jesus Christ into my life.

"Every day, I find more reasons to be thankful for what Jesus has done for me—all because of that old stranger on a street in Sydney."

On the third night, again in the sea of faces one compelled the preacher: "Sister, do you have a word for the Lord?"

With quiet manner and gentle voice, the young woman began her story. "Two years ago I visited Sydney, Australia." Once again the remarkable story was told of an old man in ragged clothes who had asked a stranger a simple question.

Two months later, the preacher went to Sydney, Australia. He wanted to find the old man. For days the preacher walked the streets of Sydney. Then, late one afternoon, an old man in ragged clothes walked up to him: "Excuse me, sir. May I ask you a question?"

The old man's name was Mr. Jenner. The preacher sat with him on a park bench and told him about the three testimonies he heard in Liverpool. Tears formed in the old man's eyes and quietly spilled down his cheeks.

He finally spoke. "More than ten years ago, I promised God I would talk to at least one person every day about Jesus Christ. In all those years I never got discouraged, but this is the first I have known that people gave their lives to the Lord because of that promise. God bless you, sir, for finding me."

Taking Aim

AUTHOR UNKNOWN

A young lady named Sally relates an experience she had in a seminary class, given by her teacher, Professor Smith, who was known for his elaborate object lessons.

One particular day, Sally walked into the seminary and knew they were in for another fun day. On the wall was a big target and on a nearby table were many darts. Professor Smith told the students to draw a picture of someone that they disliked or someone who had made them angry, and he would allow them to throw darts at the person's picture.

Sally's girlfriend drew a picture of a girl who had stolen her boyfriend. Another friend drew a picture of his little brother. Sally drew a picture of a former friend, putting a great deal of detail into her drawing, even drawing pimples on the face. Sally was pleased at the overall effect she had achieved.

The class lined up and began throwing darts, with much laughter and hilarity. Some of the students threw their darts with such force that their targets were ripping apart. Sally looked forward to her turn and was filled with disappointment when Professor Smith, because of time limits, asked the students to return to their seats.

As Sally sat thinking about how angry she was because she didn't have a chance to throw any darts at her target, Professor Smith began removing the target from the wall.

Underneath the target was a picture of Jesus…

A complete hush fell over the room as each student viewed the mangled picture of Jesus; holes and jagged marks covered His face.

Professor Smith said only these words, "In as much as ye have done it unto the least of these my brethren, ye have done it unto me."

No other words were necessary; the tear-filled eyes of each student focused only on the picture of Christ.

*And the King will answer and say to them,
"Truly I say to you, to the extent that you
did it to one of these brothers of Mine,
even the least of them, you did it to Me."*

MATTHEW 25:40

To Die For

ROSS GUNN IV
AGE 17

Tonight as I write this, the dark sky is full of stars. They seem to be letting only tiny glimpses of God flow through. I was thinking, *This is how it is when we trust God. We only see fragments of him in this dark world. But it's enough to believe that He exists and that He makes Himself known to us.*

At seventeen years old, I find myself looking up at this amazing sky and asking, "Why am I here? Would I be willing to die for something as complex and untouchable and personal as a full belief in God when He reveals Himself only in bits?"

I met this girl at a retreat a few months ago. She was telling me that she didn't think God could be real because of all the things that have happened in her life over the last few years. I sat with her, listening, and she started telling me that she had this boyfriend when she was living in England. The two of them were walking down the street one night when some guy jumped out in front of them and pulled a gun on them. She said her boyfriend stepped in front of her right when the gun went off. The robber grabbed her purse and ran, leaving her there with her dying boyfriend.

For a long time I sat there with her. I couldn't begin to imagine how awful that must have been. Finally she said, "See why it's hard for me to trust God?"

"But he's still God," I said. "He's still real."

"Yeah, well, what did God ever do for me?" she asked.

I looked at her and I knew I had to tell her what I was thinking. "I don't know if you ever realized it, but Jesus did the same thing for you that your boyfriend did. Jesus took the bullet for you. He stepped in front of you—in front of all of us at just the right time and took the bullet of sin that would have killed us. Only Jesus didn't stay dead. He came back to life and because He did, we also can live forever."

She just looked at me. After a while she said, "So what does God want from me?"

I told her that all Jesus ever wanted was the same thing her boyfriend wanted from her. He wants us to love Him back. To give ourselves to Him.

I said, "Does that sound too simple? Too easy? You've probably noticed that it isn't so simple or easy to do."

She nodded but kept listening, so I kept talking. "Things happen," I told her. "And who are we to question God why they happen? The deeper question is, do we trust God enough to love Him back no matter what? And, if so, if we're willing to confess our sins to God and make a total commitment to Him, what is that based on? Belief can't be borrowed from friends or family. It has to be yours to be real."

She walked away saying she had a lot to think about. I sat thinking about all the things I'd just heard myself say, and for the first time in my life as a Christian, I thought about how I wouldn't have been able to say all that to her if I didn't truly believe it myself.

And I do. No matter what happens, I believe. I'm committed.

Because I Care

Because I Care

Please take a moment to read the verses written on the next page. Although there are hundreds of verses in the Bible that tell us about God's love and His gift of salvation, I chose these from the book of Romans in the New Testament.

I care about what happens to you now, but I care even more about where you will spend eternity. If you have never asked Jesus Christ to be your Savior, please consider inviting Him into your life now.

Many years ago I prayed a simple prayer that went something like this…

> *Dear Jesus,*
>
> *I believe You are the Son of God and that You gave your life as a payment for the sins of mankind. I believe You rose from the dead and You are alive today in heaven preparing a place for those who trust in You.*
>
> *I have not lived my life in a way that honors You. Please forgive me for my sins and come into my life as Savior and Lord. Help me grow in knowledge and obedience to You.*
>
> *Thank You for forgiving me. Thank You for coming into my life. Thank You for giving me eternal life.*
>
> *Amen.*

If you have sincerely asked Jesus Christ to come into your life, He will never leave you or forsake you. Nothing—absolutely nothing—will be able to separate you from His love.

God bless you, dear one. I'll look forward to meeting you one day in heaven.

ALICE GRAY

For all have sinned and fall short of the glory of God.

ROMANS 3:23

For the wages of sin is death, but the gift of God
is eternal life in Christ Jesus our Lord.

ROMANS 6:23

But God demonstrated his own love toward us in this: While we
were still sinners, Christ died for us.

ROMANS 5:8

If you confess with your mouth, "Jesus is Lord," and believe in
your heart that God raised him from the dead, you will be
saved. For it is with your heart that you believe and are justi-
fied, and it is with your mouth that you confess and are saved.

ROMANS 10:9–10

Everyone who calls on the name of the Lord will be saved.

ROMANS 10:13

True Stories of Teens Living Committed Lives for Christ

Angel Award Winner!

stories for the extreme teen's heart

Celebrating Teens Who Are Saying Yes to God

Compiled by Alice Gray

Compiled with the help of teenagers, these inspiring stories show teens like you making a difference in their families, schools, and world. These compelling accounts will encourage you to a deeper walk with God, while often putting a smile on your face.

ISBN 1-57673-703-9

More Treasures for Teens

Here are inspiring stories that will touch the heart of any teen. Whether you're looking for a story about love, need a laugh, or just want an encouraging word, you'll find it in this captivating collection.

ISBN 1-57673-646-6

Let these pages become a keepsake for the favorite memories of your heart. These companion journals to *Stories for a Teen's Heart* are the perfect place to record inspirational thoughts and celebrate events that add splashes of sunshine to your life. Your writings will tell the story of a very special teenager—you!

ISBN 1-57673-705-5

New!
Journal for a Teen's Heart

A New Attitude Toward Relationships and Romance

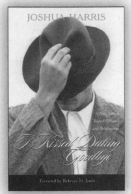

I Kissed Dating Goodbye
by Joshua Harris

Dating. Isn't there a better way? Reorder your romantic life in the light of God's Word and find more fulfillment than a date could ever give—a life of sincere singleness. Singles from 15 to 55 are tired of dating games and are ready for a new attitude toward romance. Whether you're single, dating, or divorced, this practical book can help you understand God's plan for romance in your life.

ISBN 1-57673-036-0

Boy Meets Girl
by Joshua Harris

In this dynamic sequel to *I Kissed Dating Goodbye*, newlyweds Joshua and Shannon Harris deliver an inspiring, practical illustration of how this healthy, joyous alternative to recreational dating—biblical courtship—worked for them. *Boy Meets Girl* helps readers understand how to go about pursuing the possibility of marriage with someone they may be serious about. It's the natural follow-up to the author's blockbuster book on teen dating!

ISBN 1-57673-709-8

Searching for True Love video series
by Joshua Harris

The *Searching for True Love* video series builds on the highly popular conference series and bestselling book *I Kissed Dating Goodbye* to give young adults God's direction as they seek lifetime love. Available in a three-pack or separately, the videos explore *Love*, *Purity*, and *Trust* in light of the Bible's perspective. Forty-five minutes each.

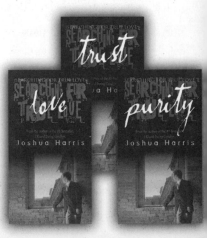

Three video series	ISBN 1-57673-645-8
Searching for True Love	ISBN 1-57673-364-2
Searching for Trust	ISBN 1-57673-643-1
Searching for Purity	ISBN 1-57673-637-7

The Heart of a Teen Speaks...

Popular Novels by Melody Carlson

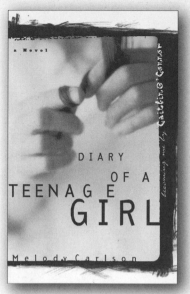

Diary of a Teenage Girl

In this compelling journal, sixteen-year-old Caitlin O'Conner explores the conflicts and joys of growing up, including her adventures with boyfriends, peer loyalty, parental conflicts, and spirituality.

ISBN 1-57673-735-7

Diary of a Teenage Girl:

Teen singing sensation **Rachael Lampa** says, "I had to keep reminding myself that I wasn't reading my own diary! It captures the thoughts and issues of a teenager's struggles to follow God's pathway."

It's My Life

In this sequel to *Diary of a Teenage Girl*, bestselling author Melody Carlson chronicles Caitlin O'Conner's day-to-day dilemmas and fulfillment as a new believer.

ISBN 1-57673-772-1

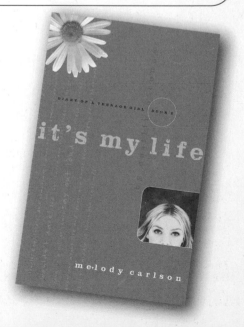

Is God doing great things in your life? In your youth group? In your community? We want to publish your real-life stories!

Send us an e-mail and we'll send you contest info that could mean cash and prizes for you or your youth group!

E-mail us at
info@amazingteenstories.com

Stories for the Heart series by Multnomah Publishers • Sisters, OR

• Love • School • Purity • Peer Pressure •
• Friends • Parents • Music • Siblings • Destiny •
• Faith • Prayer • Graduation •

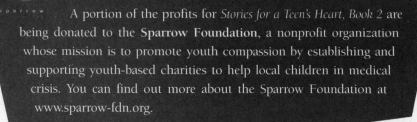

A portion of the profits for *Stories for a Teen's Heart, Book 2* are being donated to the **Sparrow Foundation**, a nonprofit organization whose mission is to promote youth compassion by establishing and supporting youth-based charities to help local children in medical crisis. You can find out more about the Sparrow Foundation at www.sparrow-fdn.org.

Acknowledgments

More than a thousand books, magazines, and other sources were researched for this collection, as well as a review of hundreds of stories sent by friends and readers of the Stories for the Heart collection. A diligent search has been made to trace original ownership, and when necessary, permission to reprint has been obtained. If I have overlooked giving proper credit to anyone, please accept my apologies. If you will contact Multnomah Publishers, Inc., Post Office Box 1720, Sisters, Oregon, 97759, corrections will be made prior to additional printings. Please provide detailed information.

Notes and acknowledgments are listed by story title in the order they appear in each section of the book. For permission to reprint any of the stories, please request permission from the original source listed below. Grateful acknowledgment is made to authors, publishers, and agents who granted permission for reprinting these stories.

REACH FOR THE STARS

"I'm Still Here" by Mary Hollingsworth. From *Hugs for Women* by Mary Hollingsworth. ©1998. Used by permission of Howard Publishing Co., Inc.

"The Letter" by Sarah Rose. © 2001. Used by permission.

"The Mark of a Champion" by Marilyn K. McAuley, copyeditor, author, and mother of a champion! © 2000. Used by permission of the author.

"I Am Loni" by Cynthia Hamond, S.F.O. © 2000. Used by permission of the author. This is the fourth Multnomah book Cynthia has been included in. She has also been published in several *Chicken Soup for the Soul* books, magazines, and one of her stories has been made for TV. You may reach her at 1021 West River St., Monticello, MN 55362 or Candbh@aol.com.

"Risking Much" by James S. Hewett. From *Illustrations Unlimited* edited by James S. Hewett © 1988. Used by permission of Tyndale House Publishers. All rights reserved.

WITH YOU ALL THE WAY

FOREVER FRIENDS

ACKNOWLEDGMENTS

live in South Carolina.

"My Forever Friend" by Kristi Powers, a stay-at-home mom who resides in Wisconsin with her husband, Michael. She loves to share from her heart about God and invites you to join the thousands of readers on their daily inspirational e-mail list: Straight From the Heart at www.MichaelTPowers.com. She can be reached via e-mail at: NoodlesP29@aol.com

"I Can't Swim" by Sara A. DuBose. © 1987. Used by permission of the author. Sara (Candy) DuBose is the author of *Conquering Anxiety* (1-800-283-1357) and appears in numerous magazines and anthologies.

"Darcy's Decision" by Teresa Cleary. © 1998. Used by permission of the author.

"Imagination Highway" by Sarah McGhehey. © 2001. Used by permission of the author.

"Dance Lessons" by Jane A. G. Kise. © 2000. Used by permission of the author. Jane Kise is a freelance writer from Minnesota. Her books include *Life Keys* and *Find Your Fit: Dare to Act on God's Design for You.*

"Getting It Right" by Molly Noble Bull. © 2000. Used by permission of the author. Her Web page is at http://mollybull.theaardvark.com

"The Invisible Signs" by Steve Lawhead, *Campus Life Magazine*. Used by permission.

"The Swing" by Teresa Cleary. ©1988. Used by permission of the author.

LOVE'S ALL IN THE FAMILY

Quote by Judy Gordon Morrow. Used by permission of the author.

"Wrinkle in My Hood" by Ken Pierpont. © 2000. Used by permission of the author. Ken Pierpont is from Fremont, Michigan. He is a pastor, conference speaker, and writer. He is the father of eight children. He publishes an electronic newsletter and can be reached by e-mail at pierpont@mail.riverview.net

"Winning Isn't Everything" by Tiffany Adams. © 2000. Used by permission of the author.

"Filling His Shoes" by Melissa Knapp. Used by permission of the author.

"Away in a Manger" by Tim Madigan. © 1997. Used by permission of the author.

"A Place of Refuge" by Melissa Marin. © 2001. Used by permission of the author. My writing helps me to express and understand who I am. I would like to thank my mom for encouraging me and Janet McHenry for believing in me.

"Weathered Love" by Nancy Simpson. © 2000. Used by permission of the author.

"Winter Nights" by Mary Slavkovsky. © 2000. Used by permission of the author.

"Dad Coming Home was the Real Treat" by Howard Mann. From the June 16, 1985, *Los Angeles Times* (Los Angeles Times Syndicate, Los Angeles, CA) © 1985. Used by permission.

"Little Sister" by Marty Wilkins. © 2001. Used by permission of the author.

"Sharing the Pain" by Nancy Gibbs. © 2000. Used by permission of the author. Nancy Gibbs is a pastor's wife and the mother of three children. She writes a weekly religious column and has been published by Honor Books, Guideposts, Chocolate for Women, Angels on Earth, and *Twins* magazine. E-mail: Daiseydood@aol.com.

"Seeing Dad through Different Eyes" by Margaret Becker. © 1996. Used by permission. Web-site: www.MaggieB.com.

KEEP LOOKING UP

"The Package Isn't Empty" by Lonni Collins Pratt. From *Here I Am, Lord* by Lonni Collins Pratt. © 1998. Permission to reproduce copyrighted material was extended by Our Sunday Visitor, 200 Noll Plaza,

YEAH, YOU MAKE A DIFFERENCE

ATTITUDE CHECK

ACKNOWLEDGMENTS

"True Courage" by Keri Schulz. © 2000. Used by permission of the author.

"Thank You, Fozzy!" by Rusty Fischer. © 2000. Used by permission of the author. Rusty Fischer is a former teacher who now writes for children. He lives with his beautiful wife, Martha, in Orlando, FL.

"The Teacher Who Knew When to Laugh" by Marti Watson Garlett. From *Kids with Character* by Marti Watson Garlett. © 1989. Used by permission of the author.

"Best Present of All" by Bonnie Compton Hanson. From *Heart Stirring Stories of Love* by Linda Evans Shepherd. © 2000. Used by permission of Broadman & Holman Publishers.

"Ahh...Life is Good" by Darah Wilson. © 2000. Used by permission of the author. Darah Wilson is a business student at Stonehill College in Easton, MA. She presented this story to two hundred professional speakers at a New England Speaker's Association's annual conference after winning the High School Speech Contest. Her e-mail is DNWilson18@aol.com.

"Like Geese Flying South" by Alan Cliburn. © 1978. Used by permission of the author. Alan Cliburn is the author of three books and hundreds of short stories.

"Blind Date" by Yitta Halberstam and Judith Leventhal. From *Small Miracles* by Yitta Halberstam and Judith Leventhal. © 1997. Used by permisson.

"A New Creation" by Christina Thuerwachter. © 2000. Used by permission of the author.

YOU KNOW WHAT'S RIGHT

"The Pre-Dawn Test" by Elaine Cunningham. Originally printed in the Jan/Feb *Christian Reader.* © 2001. Used by permission of the author.

"2:00 A.M." by D. B. From *Sons: A Father's Love* by Bob Carlisle. © 1999, Word Publishing, Nashville, Tennessee. Used by permission. All rights reserved.

"Donuts at the Back" by Wayne Rice. From *Still More Hot Illustrations for Youth Talks* by Wayne Rice. Copyright © 1999 by Youth Specialties, Inc. Used by permission of Zondervan Publishing House.

"Honesty Still Pays" by Rebecca Park Totilo. © 2001. Used by permission of the author.

"The Ride" by Kelsie Patka © 2000. Used by permission of the author.

"A Wise Maneuver" by Carole Mayhall. © 2000. Used by permission of the author.

"The Emperor's Seeds" by Wayne Rice. From *More Hot Illustrations for Youth Talks* by Wayne Rice. Copyright © 1995 by Youth Specialties, Inc. Used by permission of Zondervan Publishing House.

"Character in Action" by Barbara A. Lewis. From *What Do You Stand For? A Kid's Guide to Building Character* by Barbara A. Lewis, © 1998. Used with permission from Free Spirit Publishing Inc., Minneapolis, MN; 1-800-735-7323; www.freespirit.com. All rights reserved.

"My First Job" by Tony Hillerman. From *My First Job* by Daniel Levine. Reprinted with permission from the *Reader's Digest*, March 2000. Copyright © 2000 by The Reader's Digest Assn., Inc.

"Forward" by Christina Abt. © 2000. Used by permission of the author. Christina is a freelance writer, newspaper columnist, and radio commentator whose work has been published in a variety of books. She is a wife, mother of two, and will always be her mother's daughter.

"The Flat Tire" by Wayne Rice. From *Still More Hot Illustrations for Youth Talks* by Wayne Rice. Copyright © 1999 by Youth Specialties, Inc. Used by permission of Zondervan Publishing House.

HANG IN THERE

"Ed's Closet" by Robin Maynard. © 2000. Used by permission of the author.

"Through a Father's Eyes" by Lonni Collins Pratt. Used by permission of the author.

It's a God Thing